HORRIBLE HISTORIES

GRUESOME GUIDES

LONDON

TERRY DEARY

ILLUSTRATED BY MARTIN BROWN

D0645331

SCHOLASTIC

For Neal Foster – the Magnificent seventh. TD

To Richard Scrivener, with thanks. MB

Scholastic Children's Books,
Euston House, 24 Eversholt Street,
London NW1 1DB, UK

A division of Scholastic Ltd
London ~ New York ~ Toronto ~ Sydney ~ Auckland
Mexico City ~ New Delhi ~ Hong Kong

First published in the UK by Scholastic Ltd, 2005
(as *Horrible Histories: Loathsome London*)
This edition published 2010

Text © Terry Deary, 2005
Illustrations © Martin Brown, 2005

978 1407 10423 2

Page layout services provided by Quadrum Solutions Ltd, Mumbai, India
Printed and bound by CPI Group (UK) Ltd, Croydon, CR0 4YY

6 8 10 9 7

The right of Terry Deary and Martin Brown to be identified as
the author and illustrator of this work respectively has been asserted by
them in accordance with the Copyright, Designs and Patents Act, 1988.

CONTENTS

Introduction

Here are two cities, A and B. Which would YOU like to live in? City A?

> *I warn you! You will find all the evil of the world in that city. Do not go to the dances, do not mix with the wicked women, do not play dice, do not go to the theatre or the pub. It is full of actors, fools, villains, drug-sellers, fortune-tellers, tricksters, robbers, magicians and common beggars. If you want to keep away from evil, then stay away from this city.*

That was written around the year 1190 by a monk called Richard. He also said this place was full of 'tatterdemalions' – tramps as ragged as scarecrows.

What a place! You wouldn't want to go there, would you? It sounds like the most horrible place in history. I'm sure you'd rather live in City B...

> *Of all the great cities in the world this is the most famous. It is far greater than all the others. It has fine weather, good Christian people, strong walls, fine women and excellent men. They enjoy good sport. Their houses have beautiful gardens full of trees. Outside the city are pleasant meadows with streams of clear water. There are forests with stags, boars and wild bulls for hunting.*

That was also written around the year 1190 by a priest called William FitzStephen. William did say that this city had a problem with 'idiots who drink too much'. Apart from that it sounds a great place to live.

So travel back in time to 1190. Would you choose City A? That's Loathsome London. A disgusting and dangerous place.

Or City B? That's London too. A wonderful and charming place.

That's the trouble with history. You just don't know who to believe, do you?

6

To really get a fair and honest picture of the past you need a book that will tell you all the good AND the bad things about a piece of history. But...

> *Horrible Histories* warning: This is NOT the book to give you a fair and honest picture of London!

This book will only tell you the horrible bits of London's history – about the bad, not the brave, the horrible, not the happy, the dreadful, disgusting and dirty, not the dear, drippy and delightful.

Let's listen to people like revolting Richard and forget wet William.

Ancient London timeline

Here's a rough horrible historian's guide to ancient London. It's a mixture of the legends, the lies and the truth – historians just can't agree which is which.

Well maybe Prof B is right. An old legend says that in 1100 BC, a king called Brutus came from Troy and settled in Britain. He travelled around and finally chose a spot on the banks of the Thames to be his capital. He called it New Troy. He was buried at the White Hill – where the Tower of London is today. He defeated two giants, Gog and Magog, and took them back to London to guard the gates of the city.

The legend goes on to say that in 863 BC Bladud became King of the Britons – the people of Britain. The historian Geoffrey of Monmouth wrote:

8

> **T**his prince Bladud was a very clever Man and taught magic in his Kingdom. He also practised magic till he tried to fly to the upper Region of the Air with Wings he had made himself. He fell down upon the Temple of Apollo in the City of Trinovantium (London), where he was dashed to pieces.

This temple was probably where Westminster Abbey now stands. So if you see a red splat on a Westminster pavement you may have found the blood of Bladud.

130 BC King Lud rules in London. Lud turns New Troy into a great city with walls and palaces. It was named after him – Lud-dum. He is buried in the place we now call Ludgate. (Sounds a Lud of rubbish.)

55 BC Cassivellaunus is King of Britain and faces a new threat – the Romans are coming, led by Julius Caesar. Caesar is not welcome so he goes home after just three weeks. He leaves behind his sword, stuck in the shield of Cassivellaunus's brother. The sword is still seen in London's coat of arms. The red cross is the sign of the English saint, St George, and the dragons are the ones he killed. (Some rather boring people say it is the sword that beheaded St Paul in Rome.)

54 BC Julius Caesar is back – maybe he wants his sword. Jules charges through London and forces Cassivellaunus to make peace. But he leaves again before winter storms cut him off from his friends in France. Clever man.

AD 43 The Romans return, this time to stay for a few hundred years. But...

AD 60 Queen Boudica rebels. She destroys Colchester then burns and wrecks London.

AD 100 The Romans have rebuilt London with nice new walls to keep bad Brits like Boudica out. They also name this city the capital of Britannia. It still is.

AD 850 Now it's the Vikings' turn to trash London. They do such a good job that it won't be rebuilt till **AD 886**.

AD 961 Fire and plague in London. Not the last time these twin terrors will torment Londoners...

AD 982 The Vikings are back but THIS time the Londoners give them a good kicking. A monk wrote...

> The people of London did more slaughter
> than you would ever think city people could

Vicious for the Vikings. But their relatives will be back in…

1066 The Normans arrive … and Normans were just Vikings who had moved to northern France. Norman leader William the Conqueror is crowned at Westminster on Christmas Day. Riots and slaughter follow. Happy Christmas!

1071 A fire wrecks the wooden buildings so Will the Conk begins building the terrible Tower of London in stone.

Elephant and Castle

If the Londoners had newspapers in 54 BC the front page might have looked like this:

SPECIAL PULL-OUT PIG SECTION PART FIVE

DATE: SUMMER PRICE: A COIN

MORNING STANDARD

FREE DUCK TOKENS

DIAMOND GEEZER CAESAR SEIZES LONDON

Roaming Roman Julius Caesar has crossed the River Thames. Against all odds the Italian champ beat the brave Brit boys – and he took the trunk road!

The London legend Cassivellaunus had been attacking cool Jules for weeks and at last the Caesar had had enough. He marched up to the Thames. Of course there was only one place to cross – London. So the brainy Brits barricaded the London crossing with sharp stakes.

But the rotten Roman had the answer. He covered an elephant in armour and put a tower on its back. The jumbo creature waded through the stakes to stake his place in history. Roman soldiers sat in the tower and fired arrows and stones down on the battered Brits.

Romans crossing by Jumbo

Cassivellaunus said, 'We retreated to the woods. Some of the lads were a bit scared of the great grey beast. They're still in the woods and they don't want to come out. Ever. Looks like it's curtains for Cassivellaunus. I know when I'm beat. I plan to make peace with Caesar.'

But news is coming in that storms have wrecked much of Caesar's fleet down on the south coast. If he doesn't leave soon he'll be trapped in Britain through the winter and he won't want that. The latest reports say he's heading back as fast as his legs will carry him – or, at least, as fast as his elephant's legs will carry him.

The good old British weather comes to our rescue yet again.

Bloody Boudica

Some Brits were pleased to see the Romans – Brits who liked baths and bullying barbarians. But Big Boudica was a quaint queen who was NOT in love with the legions. She led her Iceni people to ravage the Romans. It was massacre and murder.

A horrified Roman said...

The British enjoyed robbing and nothing else. The deaths at Colchester and London were about 70,000. The British could not wait to cut throats, hang, burn and crucify.

In the smoking ruins of London you could see:
• 30,000 corpses of men, women and children
• bodies floating down the Thames
• heads cut off and stuck on poles
• bodies hanging from trees

The Romans defeated her in the end. Legend says she is now buried under platform eight of King's Cross Station. (She must be chuffed.) The place where the station was built by the Great Northern Railway in 1852 was called Battle Bridge, the site of her last battle with the Roman army.

But, before you start digging, there is another legend that says she is buried at Primrose Hill in London.

Horrible Histories note: A fine statue of Boudica and her daughters was put at the end of Westminster Bridge in 1902. The warrior queen is shown defending London ... which is a bit odd because she hated the place and tried to smash it and ash it.

Bran's brains

The Romans finally left Britain around AD 410. The country was then attacked by savage Saxons who made straight for London from northern Germany. By AD 470 the city was almost abandoned by the Brits. Britain was in the 'Dark Ages'.

Then, so they say, the famous King Arthur came along to save the south from those vicious villains the Saxons, as well as the Scots and the Irish.

Maybe you'd like to tell this Dark Ages bedtime story to a little brother or sister – a brother or sister that you want to scare so they have nightmares and wet the bed.

If you believe that stuff about Arthur ... the sword in the stone, the Round Table, the Lady of the Lake and Merlin the magician and all that ... then you may believe the story of Bran the Brit and you may believe there are fairies at the bottom of your garden.

BRAN THE BRIT

Once upon a time there was a big brave giant called Bran. Bran was not only a giant, he was also a god, so he was known as Bran the Blessed.

One day Bran took his army across to Ireland to fight the nasty Irish. Of course a giant god should have stuffed the little Irish, but Bran boobed. He only went and got himself killed, didn't he?

'Never mind,' Bran said after he was dead (gods can do tricky stuff like that), 'I want my friends to cut off my head and take it home to lovely London.'

'Won't it hurt?' one of his simple soldiers said.
'No,' Bran said. 'I'm dead.'

So they cut off his head. It was a very big head so it must have taken a lot of chopping and hacking and sawing. As they sailed back home Bran's head said, 'Bury my head beside the body of Brutus. Bury it in the White Hill. So long as my head is there then I will protect Britain. No one can invade our lovely land.'

The head was buried ... but we don't know if it kept talking after it was buried. Probably not, because the soil would get in its mouth wouldn't it? Where was I? Oh, yes. The dead head should have lived happily ever under BUT...

Along came King Arthur. 'I'm king now,' he said. 'We don't need no magic heads to look after London. That's what I'm here for lads. Dig it up.'

'You what?' they said.

'Dig it up,' he repeated. 'And dump it in the river,' he added. So that's what they did.

Was Britain invaded? Of course it was. Did Arthur's action bring a curse on the country? Of curse it did. England suffered many disasters after that.

Arthur lived unhappily ever after. Now he's buried in a magical cave somewhere. So long as he's there Britain is safe. Where have we heard that story before?

But if you ever come across a dead head floating in the river or buried under the ground – and if that dead head starts chatting, then PUT IT BACK in the White Hill.

And, when you've done that, don't forget to wash your hands.

THE END

The London mummy

In AD 634 King Cadwallon died. He was a Welsh king who had defeated the Saxons in the north.

He was not a nice man. The historian Bede said…

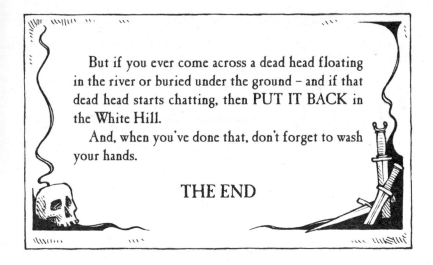

At this time there was a great slaughter both of the church and of the people of Northumbria. Cadwallon was a Christian by name but a barbarian at heart and spared neither women nor children. With beastly cruelty he put all to death by torture and for a long time raged through all their land, meaning to wipe out the whole of the English nation from the land of Britain.

ARE YOU SAXON?

CAN I THINK ABOUT IT?

Geoffrey of Monmouth said Cadwallon died peacefully of old age and was 'embalmed' – mummified. This must have been quite a sight.

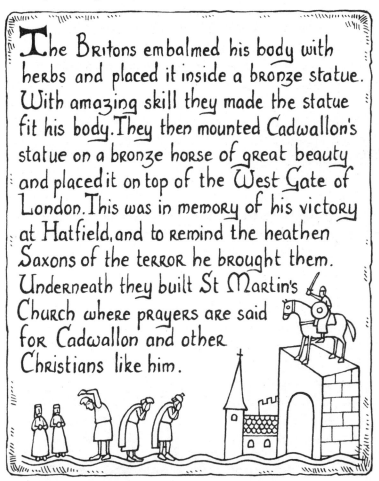

The Britons embalmed his body with herbs and placed it inside a bronze statue. With amazing skill they made the statue fit his body. They then mounted Cadwallon's statue on a bronze horse of great beauty and placed it on top of the West Gate of London. This was in memory of his victory at Hatfield, and to remind the heathen Saxons of the terror he brought them. Underneath they built St Martin's Church where prayers are said for Cadwallon and other Christians like him.

Other historians say Cadwallon was killed in battle 300 miles away. A London mummy was a bit unlikely. Cadwallon codswallop in fact.

Terrible Tower

Bran's big head may be gone but Brutus must still be buried there on White Hill. Hundreds of years later, in 1078, the Normans came along and built a castle there. It is known as 'The Tower of London' – and in the past thousand years it's had a grim, gruesome and peculiar history.

It is guarded by soldiers in fancy dress called 'Beefeaters' and by ravens. Some people believe that if those ravens ever leave the Tower then England will be destroyed. (Yes, that story again.)

But those ravens WON'T leave. Firstly because they have their big beaks stuffed with food every day, and secondly because they have their wings clipped so they can't fly.

Here are a few bird-brained facts the Beefeaters don't tell visitors…

1 The ravens are fed on rabbit meat and biscuits soaked in blood. Each raven eats about 220 g a day. That's a lot of dead bunnies. (If you want a job as a Tower raven then start eating blood-soaked biscuits for tea.)

2 The ravens are given egg once a week – which is a bit like a cannibal eating children. For a special treat they are given a whole rabbit to tear apart. If you fancy raw rabbit then you are raven mad.

3 The royal astronomer John Flamsteed told King Charles II that the birds were spoiling his work. (Probably pooping on his telescope.) The King ordered them all to be killed but he was told that would bring bad luck. Instead he said six could stay. Good luck for six ravens, bad look for Flamsteed.

4 There are supposed to be six ravens at the Tower all the time. They keep eight in case a couple fall sick and hop the twig. A bit like subs on a football team.

5 Even clipped ravens can escape. In the Second World War (1939–1945) there was just one raven left – the rest were probably driven off by the bombing.

Take your Tower terror pick

How would you like to die? If you ended up in the Tower of London then you had a lovely choice.

Which would you choose?

Beheaded

The Tower is famous as London's chopping centre, yet only seven people have been beheaded there over the years. Most victims were taken outside to Tower Hill so the people of London could watch. Over 150 died out there.

In 1601 Queen Elizabeth I's old boyfriend, the Earl of Essex, rebelled against her. She sent him to the Tower for the chop. We have a report on the event, but we don't have the Earl's story. Maybe it would look like this....

Did you know…?

If you go to the Tower of London you will see a metal sign that says…

SITE OF SCAFFOLD

Another sign gives the names of seven people who died on that spot.

Except they DIDN'T die there! The sign is a fraud.

That sign was put up because Queen Victoria wanted one to mark the place where Anne Boleyn died. But Victorian historians put the sign in the wrong place.

The truth is, Anne Boleyn got the chop in the middle of the parade ground, at least 50 metres away from the sign. The Earl of Essex and five others also died there.

Smothered

In 1483 King Edward IV died and his 12-year-old son became Edward V ... for a few weeks. But before he could be crowned, young Edward and his little brother went to the Tower and were never seen again.

Their Uncle Richard had himself crowned as Richard III – so of course he got the blame for killing them. We will never know for ccrtain if he did. But one story says the boys were smothered to death...

UNCLE RICHARD WAS EVER SO KIND. I MEAN HE DIDN'T WANT US TO SUFFER, DID HE? HE DIDN'T HAVE US CHOPPED OR BEATEN OR BURNED. NO. KIND OLD RICHARD WAITED TILL WE WERE ASLEEP AND THEN HE SENT HIS MEN TO SMOTHER US. IT WAS ALL VERY PAINLESS. THEY WRAPPED US IN OUR MATTRESSES AND HELD THEM OVER OUR FACES TILL WE COULDN'T BREATHE. IT WAS ALL OVER VERY QUICKLY. ONE OF THE KILLERS WAS CALLED WILL SLAUGHTER. WHAT A CUTE NAME FOR A MURDERER!

Nearly 200 years later, in 1674, some workmen discovered a box with the bones of two boys. Are they the bones of the missing princes? No one is sure. The bones are resting in Westminster Abbey – their gravestone says the boys were smothered with pillows.

Pillows or a mattress – the end was still the same: two kids croaked.

Stabbed

Maybe the Princes were not Richard III's first victims. In 1471 the slightly dotty King Henry VI was killed at the tower so Richard's brother Edward IV could take the throne.

There is a story that claims Richard was to blame. Richard probably didn't do it himself but it's pretty certain Henry VI died nastily...

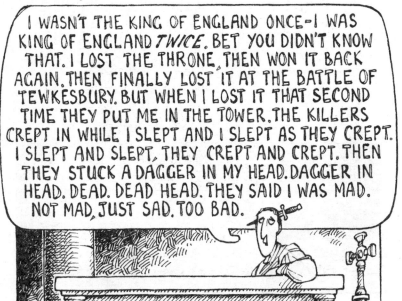

I WASN'T THE KING OF ENGLAND ONCE – I WAS KING OF ENGLAND *TWICE*. BET YOU DIDN'T KNOW THAT. I LOST THE THRONE, THEN WON IT BACK AGAIN. THEN FINALLY LOST IT AT THE BATTLE OF TEWKESBURY. BUT WHEN I LOST IT THAT SECOND TIME THEY PUT ME IN THE TOWER. THE KILLERS CREPT IN WHILE I SLEPT AND I SLEPT AS THEY CREPT. I SLEPT AND SLEPT, THEY CREPT AND CREPT. THEN THEY STUCK A DAGGER IN MY HEAD. DAGGER IN HEAD. DEAD. DEAD HEAD. THEY SAID I WAS MAD. NOT MAD, JUST SAD. TOO BAD.

Drowned

And maybe the Princes weren't even Richard's second victims. There is a story that he killed his other brother, George. Old Georgie had been a naughty boy and plotted against big brother, King Edward IV. He had to go and it was said that Richard was given the job. Maybe that's why he let George choose the execution method…

MY DEAR LITTLE BROTHER RICHARD CAME TO ME AND SAID, 'I HAVE TO EXECUTE YOU. HOW WOULD YOU LIKE TO DIE?' AND I SAID, 'OLD AGE! HA! ONLY JOKING, RICHIE OLD BRUV.' ANYWAY WE HAD A FEW DRINKS AND A BIT OF A THINK AND THAT'S WHEN I HAD THE IDEA. 'I WANT TO BE DROWNED – DROWNED IN WINE!' SO GOOD OLD RICHIE FETCHED A BARREL OF BEST MALMSEY WINE. WE DRANK HALF OF IT AND THEN HE DUNKED ME IN THE OTHER HALF. I DIED – BUT I DIDN'T WHINE ABOUT IT

CHEERS

Poisoned

Sir Thomas Overbury was not so lucky. He upset King James I and was locked up in the Tower. But his enemies decided to kill him. Slowly. Very slowly. In fact it took him six months to die.

A POWDER WAS SPRINKLED OVER MY FOOD INSTEAD OF SALT—IT WAS THE SLOW BUT DEADLY POISON ARSENIC. I HAD VOMITING AND DIARRHOEA. I ASKED FOR A CURE—THEY GAVE ME POWDER OF DIAMONDS —GROUND GLASS THAT MADE MY MOUTH AND STOMACH BLEED. THEN CANTHARADIN (FROM CRUSHED BEETLES) WAS ADDED TO MY ONION SAUCE TO CAUSE SWELLING. THEY FINISHED ME OFF WITH MERCURY POISON. THEY BURIED ME IN THE TOWER CHAPEL

Over for Overbury. King James was upset – he didn't want to get the blame for killing a prisoner. The cook was executed. Overbury must have enjoyed that!

Fallen

Oddly, some people didn't enjoy their stay at the Tower. They tried to escape. A Welsh prince, Gruffudd, was locked up by King John from 1211 till 1215. Then he was locked up by his own father in 1228 for six years. And finally he was imprisoned by his own brother in Wales in 1239 and handed over to King Henry III.

A regular little jailbird. But the Tower wasn't *that* bad. Gruff had his wife for company. And he was put in the comfortable Great Keep. Yet he tried to escape.

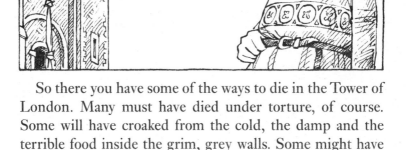

I MADE A ROPE OUT OF MY BEDCLOTHES, SOME TABLECLOTHS AND THE CURTAINS. I TIED IT TO THE END OF THE BED AND THEN I CLIMBED OUT OF THE WINDOW. ALL THESE YEARS IN PRISON MEANT I DIDN'T GET A LOT OF EXERCISE. AND I ATE RICH FOOD IN THE TOWER. WHAT I'M TRYING TO SAY IS, I WAS A BIT HEAVY. ALL RIGHT I WAS *FAT*. AND BOY SCOUTS HADN'T BEEN INVENTED BACK IN 1244. MY KNOTS WERE USELESS. MY ROPE PARTED AND I FELL. I BROKE MY NECK. STILL, I DIDN'T DIE IN PRISON AS MY ENEMIES WANTED!

So there you have some of the ways to die in the Tower of London. Many must have died under torture, of course. Some will have croaked from the cold, the damp and the terrible food inside the grim, grey walls. Some might have even died of the deadliest killer of all – old age.

Which would you choose?

Did you know…?
One of the horriblest London deaths was that of Richard the Raker. And it didn't happen at the Tower. Richard's job was to rake the poo out of the toilet pits. These smelly pits lay under London houses and they filled up fast.

In 1326 Richard the Raker slipped and fell into a pit. He couldn't swim. A writer at the time said…

He was sitting on the latrine in his own house and the rotten planks gave way, and he fell in and drowned monstrously in his own sewage.

So be careful next time you visit the boys' toilets at your school. (Sorry, I have no knowledge of the girls' toilets. Surely they can't be as bad?)

Middle Ages London timeline

London in the Middle Ages was smelly. People emptied their toilet pots into the street. Still, a piddle shampoo was not the worst thing that happened to people in Middle Ages London.

1189 Richard I is crowned. Loathsome Londoners celebrate by murdering 30 Jewish merchants. A story had gone around that Richard had ordered their massacre. He hadn't. It was all a big mistake. Oooops! It's their idea of fun.

1196 William Fitz Osbert kills the Archbishop of Canterbury's guard and is hanged at Tyburn (Hyde Park Corner today). He is the first of around 50,000 who will be hanged at Tyburn over the centuries.

1261 Henry III is at war with his barons (led by Simon de Montfort). Henry hides in the Tower as Italian monks are murdered in the streets. Queen Eleanor is stoned by Londoners. She has to shelter in St Paul's Cathedral. When Henry finally wins in 1265, de Montfort's supporters are punished.

1305 William Wallace, Scottish rebel, is hanged, drawn and quartered in London … that's to say hanged till he was half dead, slit open so his guts could be drawn from his body and thrown on a fire, then beheaded and cut into quarters. Wallace's death is very slow – long-drawn-out, in fact.

1338 Attacks from France and poor harvests mean starvation for many in the south. In London, people are trampled to death in queues for bread. There are even reports of cannibalism. Loathsome – but luscious – Londoners.

1348 Plague arrives.

1381 An army of peasants from Kent and Essex march on London. They do something no one has done before or since – they capture the Tower of London. The Archbishop of Canterbury and the King's treasurer are killed. The King, Richard II, is only 14 at the time but tricky young Dicky has their leader killed. They give up and go home. End of a pleasant peasant holiday in London.

The Black Death

Fleas carry the plague from rats to humans. Don't blame the poor little rats! They catch the plague and die too.

For three or four days you feel fine. Then you start to sweat, can't sleep, shake and throw up. By the next day you have a terrible headache, feel dizzy, can't stand bright light and have pain in your gut and legs. On the third day your eyes become bloodshot and your tongue swells and turns white. This later goes brown or yellow. You get swellings under your arms, on your neck or at the tops of your legs. Death follows soon after.

Of course there were cures. The priests said wicked people caught the plague – so say your prayers. They also gave this advice:

Do not eat chicken, duck, goose or fish

Do not eat pig, old beef or fat meat

Do not sleep during the daytime

Do not take too much exercise

Do not cook anything in rainwater

Do not have a bath

WHAT AM I DOING HERE? I CAN'T READ

They seemed to think anything touched by water was a danger. Wrong!

Do not think of death, think of pleasant things

Visit beautiful gardens and look at lovely scenery

Smell fresh flowers and listen to sweet music

Look at gold, silver and jewels

Wrong again!

In London they believed loud noises would drive the plague away. They rang church bells (till the bell ringers died of plague) and even fired cannon.

You'd probably be pleased to catch plague to get some peace.

Poll-taxed,[1] poll-axed

In the 1300s the English people were told to pay extra tax. This was to cover the cost of wars in France. Everyone over the age of 15 on the council's list of names had to pay, except monks, nuns and priests.

In 1377 over 1,250,000 people paid.

In 1380 only 800,000 people paid.

If you are any good at sums then you will know 450,000 people 'disappeared' in three years.

1 A 'Poll' is a head so a 'poll tax' was a tax on heads ... if you have a head then you are taxed. If you have no head then you are not taxed. If you want to dodge the tax then simply leave your head in bed. No one will notice.

Was it the plague? No.

Was it alien kidnappers? No.

These people went into hiding to dodge their taxes.

In 1381 the peasants marched on London to sort out the young King Richard II. They wanted to tell him how unfair this tax was – the poor paid as much as the posh. It was called 'The Peasants' Revolt'. Apart from robbing and burning the homes of rich people the peasants did something quite shocking. Thomas Walsingham reported...

The peasants headed for the royal rooms at the Tower of London. Who would believe it but this mob dared to enter the rooms of the King and his mother with their filthy sticks. They lay and sat on the King's bed. Several asked the King's mother to kiss them.

The King's chief tax collector, Hales, was dragged out to Tower Hill where his head was lopped off and stuck on London Bridge. (The skull ended up in a cupboard in a Suffolk house and it's still there.)

The rebels also broke open the London prisons and set the criminals free. The warden of Southwark Prison ran for cover to Westminster Abbey. Holy buildings were supposed to be 'safe' places. But the rebels dragged him out and lopped off his head too.

London Bridge must have been filling up! Wonder if they had a warning sign?

  MIND YOUR HEAD

How did it all end? A book of the time said…

Afterwards the King sent out his messengers into the country to capture the rebels and put them to death. And many were taken and hanged at London and they set up many gallows around the City of London. At last, as it pleased God, the King took pity in his heart, and gave them all pardon, saying that they should never rise again or they would lose their lives or limbs. He gave them a deed but they had to pay the King twenty shillings each to make him rich. And so finished this wicked war.

So Little Dicky came out of it quite well!

Not the Dick Whittington story

Dick Whittington is famous. The pantomime story says he was heading for London to seek his fortune but lost heart. He was heading home when the bells rang out and called, 'Turn again Whittington!' He turned back, made his fortune (with the help of his rat-catching cat), married the beautiful girl and lived happily ever after.

Of course London people WOULD tell that story – 'Come to London and get rich!' is the message.

Let's face it, 'Come to London and get plagued, imprisoned, bombed or beheaded' is more likely. But then no one at all would go to London and Sunderland would become capital of England.

The TRUTH about Richard Whittington (1350–1423) is a bit more boring:

- He DIDN'T take a cat to London.
- He trained as a cloth merchant and made his money by lending money to the King.
- King Richard II forced London to take Rich Whittington as mayor.

The cat story was made up 200 years after Rich Richie had gone to his grave. A stone at Highgate Hill showed where he was supposed to have turned back to London. In 1964 the cat was added to the stone.

The Real Richard married Alice Fitzwarren, but they died with no children. He left his money for the good of London. What sort of goodies did the lucky Londoners get?

a) public toilets
b) prisons
c) a home for cats

Answer: a) and b) ... so, next time you have a widdle in a London toilet, say 'Thank you, Dick!'

But there is another story that tells how a man from Swaffham in Norfolk made his fortune by LEAVING London. It's just as likely as the Dick Whitandcat pantomime story. Here is the 'Panto of the Poor Peasant Farmer'…

A farmer from Swaffham had a strange dream

ON LONDON BRIDGE JUST WAIT AROUND.
YOU'LL HEAR OF GOLD BELOW THE GROUND!
GO THERE NOW AND DO NOT DITHER,
DO NOT WANDER HITHER-THITHER

So off he went to London where he shivered on the bridge

HERE I BE ON THE BORING BRIDGE.
I MAY AS WELL STAND IN A FRIDGE!
STILL I'LL WAIT FOR THIS GOOD NEWS
WHILE THE WIND BLOWS UP MY TREWS...
...ERS

1 Fridges have not been invented,
For this tale let's just pretend it.
Why is this all done in rhyme?
'Cos it is a pantomime...
...stupid.

34

YOU WATCHING ME YOU SMELLY PEST?
I MAY JUST CALL FOR YOUR ARREST.
LONDON TOWN IS FULL OF DANGERS,
WE HATE PEDLARS, WE HATE STRANGERS

So the farmer told him...

I DON'T MEAN NO HURT OR HARM
I'VE JUST COME DOWN FROM ME FARM.
I HAVE HAD A DREAM OF GOLD.
STANDING HERE I WILL BE TOLD...
...WHERE IT IS

The shopkeeper laughed and sneered, sneered and laughed

I HAVE DREAMS LIKE THAT QUITE OFTEN.
MINE TELL ME TO GO TO SWAFFHAM!
THERE BENEATH AN OLD PEAR TREE
A POT OF GOLD I'LL SURELY SEE...
...BELIEVE THAT AND YOU'LL BELIEVE
ANYTHING!

Which just goes to prove that old English proverbs are right. You know the ones ... a friend in need is a pain in the neck, a bird in the hand will poo in your palm, and red sky at night means your eyes are probably bloodshot.

Did you know...?
Londoners have had some odd ideas. Cats like their home and, if the owners move, the cats won't stay in the new house. How did a Londoner get a cat to stay at a new home in the Middle Ages? Picked it up by the tail and swung it once around the room. And that's a true tale. (The cat was probably too dizzy to find the door after that.)

Awful for animals

In prehistoric times – before London was built – there must have been sharks in Soho and wolves in Wapping, crocodiles snapping in Shoreditch and hyenas – who probably just came for a good laugh.

Then London was built. London has been a horrible place for many humans. It has also been awful for animals.

There was…

Bear-baiting

London had bear-gardens since the time of Henry II (1154–1189). A bear would have its teeth and claws removed, then it was chained to a post by a back leg or by the neck. Trained dogs were sent to attack it. This was called 'baiting'.

The Dutch scholar Erasmus, writing about 1500, said…

There are many herds of bears kept in England just to be baited. Sunday is the favourite day for these sports.

ARE WE A HERD?

FIRST I'VE HEARD

Hentzner, a German traveller writing in 1598, described the bear-garden at Bankside in London as a sort of a theatre for the baiting of bulls and bears.

It sometimes happens they are killed on the spot; fresh ones are immediately supplied in the place of those that are wounded or tired.

I'M POOPED

He also describes the whipping of a blinded bear for 'fun'. A famous baiting took place before Queen Elizabeth in 1575, for which 13 bears were provided. Richard Laneham was amongst the guests. He wrote:

> *It was a very pleasant sport to see. To see the bear, with his pink eyes, tearing after his enemies; the nimbleness and cunning of the dog against the strength and experience of the bear: if he were bitten then see him get free with biting, with clawing, with roaring, with tossing and tumbling; and when he was loose to shake his ears two or three times with the blood and the slaver hanging about his face.*

Bull-baiting

It wasn't just bears that suffered and died in the bear-pits of London. Bulls did too. A hundred years after Elizabeth baited her last bear it was still going on ... but not everyone enjoyed it so much. Some even felt sorry for the animals. John Evelyn wrote in his now-famous Diary in 1670:

> *I went with some friends to the bear-garden, where there was cock-fighting, dog-fighting, bear and bull-baiting, it being a famous day for all these butcherly sports, or rather barbarous cruelties. The bulls did exceedingly well, but the Irish wolf-dog was best when it beat a cruel mastiff. One of the bulls tossed a dog into a lady's lap, as she sat in one of the boxes quite high above the arena. Two poor dogs were killed, and it all ended with the ape on horseback. I am most heartily weary of these crude and dirty pastimes.*

By the 1800s people were trying to ban these sports. But when Tsar Nicholas I of Russia visited England he was taken to see a bull-baiting.

The bull's nose was blown full of pepper to drive it wild. Tricks to make a bear mad included putting dried peas in its ear or tying fireworks to its back.

Bear-baiting and bull-baiting were banned by law in 1835. Many people ignored the ban and went ahead anyway. There was a bull-baiting event at London's Agricultural Hall in 1870.

So much for the law.

Cock-fighting

Cock-fighting was banned in 1849 (but still goes on in London, in secret, today).

Sometimes fighting cockerels are pecked to death. Sometimes their hearts are stabbed by sharp spurs fastened to claws.

Dog-fighting

Dog-fighting was also banned but still goes on today. In London in the 1800s you could get advice on how to train your dog to kill ... and win fights and make you money.

A writer in the 1850s complained you couldn't get to see many dog-fights in pubs, like you could in the old days. But there were plenty of dog-fights in the homes of rich men, where they were hidden from the law.

Horse and pony-baiting

From time to time there was horse-baiting in London. On one occasion the horse actually won. The crowd was furious and tore tiles off the roof of the theatre till the horse was brought back and attacked by more dogs.

The crowd wasn't happy till the horse was dead.

The Paris Garden in Southwark was the chief bear-garden in London. A Spanish nobleman of the 1580s was taken to see a pony baited. The pony had an ape tied to its back.

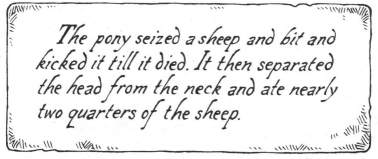

The animal was kicking amongst the dogs, while the ape clung to its back and screamed. The dogs hung from the ears and neck of the pony. It was very laughable.

We do not know what the pony thought of it.

In 1790 a pony was trained to kill sheep for 'sport'. The report said…

The pony seized a sheep and bit and kicked it till it died. It then separated the head from the neck and ate nearly two quarters of the sheep.

Today this sort of thing would get you barred from the Pony Club.

(Or baa-ed.)

Badger-baiting

When bear-baiting became illegal some cruel London 'sportsmen' turned to killing badgers with dogs. In the 1700s they would nail a badger's tail to the floor then set dogs to kill it.

Bad for bunnies

Regent's Park Zoo is a popular place to visit in London. In the 1870s you could see the boa constrictor snake being fed ... with a live rabbit.

The writer William Thackeray was horrified. He said...

Yes – swallowing a live rabbit, sir, and looking as if he would have swallowed one of my little children after it.

IT'S PAGE 18 ALL OVER AGAIN

That would stop them rabbitting on.

Terrible Tudor and slimy Stuart timeline

London in the Middle Ages was dangerous, dirty and disgusting. Then along came the Tudors and, boy, did things change!

Er … no, actually, they didn't. You lovers of the lousy side of London will be pleased to know the Horrible Henries and the Smelly Stuarts were simply differently disgusting…

1517 The loathsome Londoners are fed up with Italian bankers having all the money. They plan to massacre them on May Day. But the government catches some rebels and has them hanged, drawn and quartered. The hangman invents a scaffold on wheels so he can take it round London and give everyone a look. One writer says, 'They were just poor younglings.' So, Henry VIII had kids executed.

1587 Plotters plan to kill Queen Elizabeth I and put Mary, Queen of Scots on the English throne. The plotters are captured and taken to Holborn to be executed horribly – hanged till they are half dead then have their guts and naughty bits cut off and thrown on a fire in front of their eyes. Their deaths were so cruel even Queen Elizabeth was shocked.

1603 Old Mother Shipton dies up in Yorkshire. But she has seen into the future and says, 'London in 66 will be burned to ashes.' Sixty-six minutes? Sixty-six years time? Or in 1666? We'll have to wait and see.

1642 King Charles I has a row with Parliament and goes to war with it. Charlie's chaps (Cavaliers) battle with Parliament's people (Roundheads). In this English Civil War London is the place for protest. London women march for peace. Soldiers fire blanks to try to scare them – the women laughed. So the soldiers fire real bullets, kill a woman, and the laughing stops. One woman has her nose cut off in the fighting and an old woman is arrested for waving a rusty sword. She is carried off with her hands tied behind her back. A dangerous dame?

1649 Charles I has his head lopped off at Whitehall – outside the banqueting hall. It's enough to put you off your banquet! That's what he gets for fighting against people power.

1659 At Enfield the army officers are taking over the 'common' land – the place where the village people graze

their cattle – to plant corn. The army thinks its corn is more important than the commoners' cows. The villagers have nowhere for their animals and are furious. So they break down the new fences and let their cows trample and eat the corn. The army sends in 15 soldiers. They are attacked by 150 villagers. A report at the time described the scene…

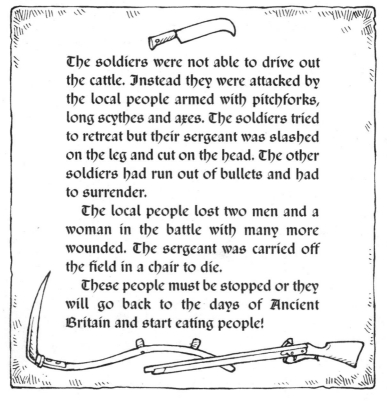

The soldiers were not able to drive out the cattle. Instead they were attacked by the local people armed with pitchforks, long scythes and axes. The soldiers tried to retreat but their sergeant was slashed on the leg and cut on the head. The other soldiers had run out of bullets and had to surrender.

The local people lost two men and a woman in the battle with many more wounded. The sergeant was carried off the field in a chair to die.

These people must be stopped or they will go back to the days of Ancient Britain and start eating people!

1665 Plague kills 70,000 Londoners. It kills even more of the poor little rats that spread it. They are saved when…

1666 London's burning. It is still a city of wood and wattle. When a fire starts in a baker shop at Pudding Lane it burns down most of the old city, 13,200 houses and St Paul's Cathedral. Some say it is a curse from the ghost of King Charles I – why did he wait 17 years? Some say it is Mother Shipton's magical forecast come true.[1]

The Dorchester Old Man – 1665

Every single person who ever lived in London has a story to tell. But some are more tragic than others. This one is horrible – and horribly sad…

> We'll never know his name, only that he came from London.
>
> The streets were empty that hot summer – except for the rats and the corpses. The people were dying faster than they could bury them. Huge pits were filled with corpses and covered over.
>
> Fresh corpses were stacked in the streets, waiting. They swelled and they smelled till the carters came and carried them away.

1 Great guess Mother S. But she also said the world would end in 1881. We're still waiting.

The old man looked around the bare room with wooden walls and a cool stone floor. His wife lay on the filthy straw mattress, her face twisted with the last pains. A dead rat lay at her feet.

He scratched and shuffled to the door. 'Goodbye, girl,' he muttered as he opened the door gently and let in the heat from the street. The door was decorated with a roughly painted red cross. 'They'll stop me if they catch me, you know,' he said to his wife. She didn't reply.

The street was empty. He took one last look. 'Someone will be along to ... to see to you soon,' he promised. 'Goodbye.'

The old man clutched the bundle of food and a few coins to his skinny chest. He blinked in the sun and limped down the street on his thin-soled shoes. He turned his face away from the pitiful pile of bodies at the corner of the street.

Somewhere a bell clacked and a voice croaked, 'Bring out your dead!'

'You'll have to go and get her,' he muttered and turned towards the west.

By the time the sun was setting he was out of the stinking city. He sat beneath a hedge, breathed the grassy air and felt better.

After a few bites of the dry bread from his pack he curled up and fell asleep. In the dark his dreams were haunted by visions of bodies, bloated and blue-spotted. He saw devils coming to haul him away to Hell and throw him into a bottomless burial pit. He screamed and woke.

The man licked some dew off the grass to quench his thirst and rose stiffly to his feet. He shook his ragged clothes and coughed. 'Not dead yet, then,' he croaked and set off with the warm morning sun on his back.

Before he'd gone a mile, a wagon of hay passed him. 'Going far?' the driver asked.

'Dorchester,' the old man said. 'That's where I was born. That's where I might as well die.'

The carter reached down a hand and pulled the old man up alongside him. 'I'm headed that way,' he said.

They travelled for two days before they reached the ancient town. The old man remembered the great church but so much else had changed. He remembered the laughing faces of his childhood. Now there were scowls and spitting hatred.

'We're a clean town here,' a woman said and waved a wooden cross at him. 'We don't want your London plague pests here. Get out!' she cried. 'Get out!'

A crowd began to gather at the market square. 'I'm not from London,' the old man whined.

'Liar!' the woman said – and she was right.

He stretched out a shaking hand. 'I have money.'

'All the money in the world won't buy you a place in Dorchester,' she snarled. She bent down and picked up a stone. 'Get out of our town,' she spat.

He staggered out of the town as the people showered him with stones and curses. At last he found an old shepherd's hut with tumbling wattle walls and a storm-blown roof. It stood on the edge of a steep quarry. He sank on the cool earth floor and curled up.

That night the sweating started. Then the pain in the armpits. His head burned with fever. He wanted water, but he was too weak to drink it.

He slept and dreamed. He woke ... and thought he was still dreaming. The hut was moving. In the morning light he could see clearly now through his crusted eyes. He could feel the wall of the hut pushing at him. It rolled him forward.

The old man heard the people of Dorchester grunting and hissing with effort. 'Ten more feet,' someone whispered. 'Push ... for God's sake, push!'

The old man rolled forward. The hut began to tilt as it reached the edge of the quarry. It hung in the air like a hawk. Then like a hawk it toppled forward and down, faster and faster. It swept the old man to his death in the quarry below.

The Dorchester woman dusted her hands. 'A quicker death than the disease,' she said. 'We did him a favour.' No one answered. No one looked at her. They kept their eyes on the ground as they hurried back to their homes.

The woman looked over the edge. 'It wasn't murder – we had to save ourselves. It wasn't murder,' she said to the empty air. 'Not really.'

She never knew his name. Only that he came from London.

London's burning

Back in 1605 people worried that the Catholics were going to take over the country when Guy Fawkes plotted to blow up the King. In 1667 they *still* feared the Catholics and so the Catholics got the blame for burning down London in the Great Fire.

A mad Frenchman called Robert Hubert *said* he had started the fire – even though he hadn't. And, of course, the French were Catholics. He was sentenced to hang. A report of the day gave the gruesome details...

The night before his execution Hubert ate dinner while people of London paid to watch him. The next day (29 October) he went in a parade to the gallows. In front of him was a large model of the Pope. The head of the Pope was filled with live cats. At the scaffold the Pope was set on fire. The Pope screamed as the cats burned and everyone was delighted. Hubert was hanged by Jack Ketch and his body was torn apart by the Londoners who went to watch.

When the writer says 'everyone was delighted' he did not mean the cooked cats were delighted – they were a–lighted.

Cool for criminals

Over the centuries thousands of horrible people have lived in London. Here are a few you would NOT want to invite round for tea…

NAME: *Bloody Bonner (real name Bishop Edmund Bonner) 1500–1569*

DETAILS: *Catholic then Protestant then Catholic Bishop – whatever was best for him*

NOTES:

Mary Tudor wanted Protestants burned alive. Bonner was the man to catch them and burn them. He was quite happy to have children executed. Bonner tried to get men like Thomas Thomkins (a weaver) to become Catholic in 1556. When Tommy Thom refused his hands were burned over candles. When he still refused Bloody Bonner sent him to be burned all over at Smithfield. The beastly bishop held his burnings on holidays so all London could come and watch the fun. He had hundreds executed. He died unloved, buried at midnight so avenging enemies wouldn't try to destroy the coffin.

MIGHT SAY: *'Come on, baby, light my fire.'*

NAME: Richard Topcliffe
1532-1604

DETAILS: Queen Elizabeth I's
torturer-in-chief in the 1590s

NOTES: One member of Parliament said that
Topcliffe was so friendly with the Queen he had
seen her legs and knees. He enjoyed whipping, burning,
chopping and stretching Catholic priests. He liked to
stand them on a stool, hang them by the wrists with
chains, then take the stool away. He even built a
torture chamber at his own home in Westminster.

MIGHT SAY: 'I like to "rack" my brains to think
of new tortures!'

NAME: George Abbott
1562-1633

DETAILS: Archbishop of
Canterbury

NOTES: When a preacher disagreed with him
Archbishop George had him whipped 36 times
and put in the pillory for hours on a freezing
November day. There the preacher had his face
branded, his nose slit and his ears cut off before
he was sent to prison. Then the Archbishop shot
a man with an arrow. King James agreed that
the victim shouldn't have got in the way of the
Archbishop's arrow. George was not punished.

MIGHT SAY: 'That'll teach the idiot to walk in
front of a loaded bow.'

NAME: *Moll Cutpurse (real name Mary Frith) 1584 – 1659*

DETAILS: *Queen of thieves, pickpocket turned gang-leader*

NOTES: *Tomboy as a child, grew up as tough and crafty as any man to become London's top thief. When she stole a farmer's watch he had her arrested. The constable took the watch to court – but when he got there he found the watch had been pinched from his pocket. She was set free. She was arrested for dressing as a man and her hobby was training dogs to kill bears in the bear garden.*

MIGHT SAY: *'When I'm around you have to "watch" yourself.'*

NAME: Jack Ketch 1663–1686

DETAILS: London executioner

NOTES: The clumsiest axeman in history. He took at least eight chops to get the Duke of Monmouth's head off in 1685. After chop one Monmouth looked up and after chop three Ketch threw his axe away. Monmouth told him to get on with it. Ketch had to finish off the job with a knife. (The head was later stitched back on so Monmouth's corpse could have its picture painted.)

MIGHT SAY: 'Ooops! Sorry, I'll try again. Ooops! And again! Ooooops!'

NAME: Catherine Hayes - died 1726

DETAILS: Landlady of a tavern called 'The Gentleman in Trouble'

NOTES: In 1726 she cut off her husband's head and threw it into a bucket. She then scattered other bits of his body around London. The head was found and stuck on a pole in a London churchyard;[1] a sign said, 'Do you know who this belongs to?' Cruel Cath was arrested and sentenced to death. But the punishment for killing a husband wasn't hanging – it was burning alive. She was one of the last women ever to be burned at Tyburn.

MIGHT SAY: 'I'll be the toast of the town.'

NAME: Thomas Henry Hocker - died 1845

DETAILS: Murderer of James Delarue, February 1845

NOTES: Tom Henry dressed in his long black coat, went out and killed James Delarue. Most people would run away. But terrible Tom hung around. When a policeman discovered the body Tom sprang out from behind some trees, singing to himself. He then began to chat to the policeman and said 'It's a nasty job,' and took hold of the dead man's hand. He was hanged!

MIGHT SAY: 'I'm a killer, you're a bobby. Ooooh, this is a nasty jobby. Tra-la-la.'

---

1 They gave it a good scrub first so it didn't look too horrible. Bet you're pleased about that.

NAME: *The London Monster*
around 1789-90

DETAILS: *Attacked, stabbed and slashed London women in the street*

NOTES: *A charming man who asked a lady to smell his flowers. But the flowers hid a spike that he jabbed in her face. His other method was to hide in bushes, jump out and stab a lady in the bum. A maker of paper flowers, Rhynwick Williams, was arrested and the attacks stopped. But many people believed he was innocent.*

MIGHT SAY: *'The police will never get to the bottom of the mystery – but I ALWAYS get to the bottom!'*

NAME: Jack the Ripper
around 1888

DETAILS: Murdered at least six women.

NOTES: His victims were cut up by someone who seemed to know how the human body is put together. A doctor, perhaps? The killer sent letters to the police and named himself 'Jack the Ripper'. Police Chief Charles Warren trained bloodhounds to catch Jack – but ended up being chased across Tooting Common by his own hounds! Most likely suspect is lawyer Montague John Druitt. He drowned himself in the Thames ... the murders stopped.

MIGHT SAY: 'Never caught. I had a few slices of luck.'

Quaint and quirky vile villains

London has seen some quaint and cruel criminal activity through its history. Here are a few examples...

1 Body for sale

In the 1700s the corpses of hanged men could be handed over to doctors for cutting up. The idea was that the surgeons could show students how the inside of a body worked. It was also a horrible 'extra' punishment for the criminal.

In April 1739 a shoemaker was hanged and then carried off to the surgeons. But his kind friends rescued his body and took it back to his widow.

She didn't want it!

The body-snatchers tried to sell it (very cheaply) to London surgeons.

USUALLY TEN POUNDS – BUT I'M NOT ASKING TEN POUNDS – I'M NOT EVEN ASKING FIVE. TO YOU, SIR, SPECIAL OFFER TODAY, ONE FRESH CORPSE, ONLY TWO POUNDS. YES, TWO POUNDS. TELL YOU WHAT, I'LL EVEN THROW IN AN EXTRA LEG FOR FREE!

No one wanted it.

They dumped the body in a shallow grave in St George's Fields.

2 Thieves' vinegar

When the Black Death came to London in 1349 the thieves had a great time. They just walked into the houses of the plague victims and robbed them. (If you have died from the plague you are not going to stop them, are you?)

After a time people noticed that the thieves never seemed to catch the plague themselves. They asked the thieves...

So the doctors started to sell this idea to people scared of catching the plague.

It seemed to work.

3 Pedal power and policemen

London policemen were given exams to see if they knew the law. The exams were not written – the policemen were not very good at writing. Instead they were spoken. The policeman had to learn the answers off by heart.

Some of the crimes that took place in London were quite shocking. Here are some of the test questions from 1864 … can you guess the answers?

Replace the *!?#! with the correct answer.

a) IS IT A CRIME IF THE RIDER OF A BICYCLE RIDES IN A FURIOUS AND A RECKLESS MANNER AND KNOCKS DOWN AND INJURES A PERSON? *!?#!

b) IS IT AN OFFENCE TO DISTURB SOMEONE IN A HOUSE BY RINGING THE DOOR BELL OR KNOCKING WITHOUT A GOOD REASON? *!?#!

c) IF A NUMBER OF PEOPLE BOO AND HISS A PLAY OFF THE STAGE CAN THEY BE CHARGED? *!?#!

d) FROM WHERE MAY A POLICEMAN MOVE A DEAD BODY? *!?#!

e) WHAT WOULD YOU DO IF A BUILDING COLLAPSED BURYING SEVERAL PEOPLE INSIDE? *!?#!

Did you know…?

The first police were on London's streets in 1829. The first dead policeman was on the streets less than a year later.

Constable Grantham tried to arrest two drunks in north London and was kicked to death.

4 Highway to heaven

Jack Collett (1659–1691) robbed people on the road. But curious Collett liked to carry out the robberies dressed as a bishop.

One night he lost his bishop's clothes in a card game. He set out to rob a coach so he could buy some new priestly clothes.

Who did he happen to stop? The Bishop of Winchester.

HEAVEN SENT

Not only did he nick the Bishop's clothes but a purse of fifty gold pieces too.

Jolly Jack was later caught breaking into a Smithfield church to rob it and was hanged at Tyburn.

5 Dive for gold

A London pickpocket was known as a 'diver'.

In the early 1700s Mary Young was so good at picking pockets she was known as 'Jenny Diver'. This Irish woman practised for two hours a day till she was an expert. One of her tricks was to wait at the bottom of the steps at a church. As a rich gentleman walked past she would hold out her hand so he could help her up the steps. When she let go of his hand his wedding ring would be missing.

And she even made a special costume to help her pocket-picking pilfering. Here's what she did ... do NOT try this at home.

Jenny Diver was caught and 'transported' to the prison colony in Virginia, America. A rich friend paid for her to sail back to London.

She was caught again, transported again and went back to London again.

She was caught again … and hanged.

This time she didn't go back.

6 Hanging around

It was Christmas Eve 1705. On the day you hang up your Christmas stocking, John Smith was hanging by the neck at Tyburn prison. He was a housebreaker who had been sentenced to die on the scaffold.

Christmas Eve is not a nice day to die … and John Smith DIDN'T die. After he'd been hanging for quarter of an hour a pardon arrived. The executioner cut the rope.

John Smith told his story…

I remember a great pain caused by the weight of my body. My spirits were in a great uproar, pushing upwards; when they got into my head I saw a great blaze of glaring light that seemed to go out of my eyes with a flash. Then the pain went.

When I was cut down I got such pins-and-needles pains in my head that I could have hanged the people who set me free.

MERRY CHRISTMAS

BAH, HUMBUG!

John became known as 'Half-hanged Smith'.

But he hadn't learned his lesson. He was arrested two more times for hanging crimes. The first time he was set free.

The second time he looked doomed. The judge was about to send Half-hanged to be fully hanged when Smith's luck struck again. The judge dropped down dead. Smith went free.

They should have changed his name again – to 'Lucky' Smith.

7 Shoplifter shopped

Mary Jones had two young children. In 1770 her husband was dragged off to fight in the navy ('press-ganged') leaving Mary penniless.

Mary Jones went into a shop on Ludgate Street and slipped some cloth under her coat. When the shopkeeper saw her she put the cloth back. So, really, she stole nothing.

Still she was arrested and taken to court. She spoke up for herself...

I was never in debt till my husband was press-ganged. Now I've no bed to lie on, nothing to give my children to eat and they are almost naked. I may have tried to take the cloth — I hardly knew what I was doing.

The law officers spoke up for her...

WHAT SHE SAYS IS TRUE. HER HUSBAND IS FIGHTING IN THE FALKLANDS AND SHE FELL INTO DEBT. SHE TRIED SELLING FURNITURE TO BUY FOOD BUT NOW IT'S ALL GONE, SHE IS NOT A CRIMINAL

So, of course, she should have been set free and helped. But the shopkeepers of Ludgate Street had other ideas...

WE ARE SICK AND TIRED OF SHOPLIFTERS. WE WANT HER PUNISHED AS HARSHLY AS THE LAW WILL ALLOW

EVEN IF THAT MEANS HANGING HER?

YESSS!

Mary Jones was hanged. She was 18 years old.

8 Taking turns

For 800 years criminals were hanged at Tyburn. The 'gibbet' was a triangle (see below) and eight people could be hanged from each side – 24 at once.

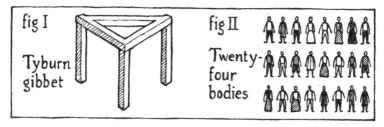

fig I

Tyburn gibbet

fig II

Twenty-four bodies

For the first 300 years they climbed ladders with ropes around their necks. The ladders were taken away and they choked on the ropes. Twisting the ladder away was called 'turning off' a criminal.

Later a cart was used. A Swiss visitor, Cesar de Saussure, wrote about it in the 1720s...

On the day of execution the prisoners, wearing a sort of white linen shirt over their clothes and a cap on their heads, are tied two together and placed on carts with their backs to the horses' tails. These carts are guarded and surrounded by officers on horseback, each armed with a sort of pike.

One often sees criminals going to their deaths quite carefree, others so shameless that they fill themselves full of liquor and mock at those who are in misery. When all the prisoners arrive at Tyburn they are made to climb onto a very wide cart. A cord is passed round their necks and the end fastened to the gibbet, which is not very high. The priest who is also on the cart makes them pray and sing a few verses of hymns. The relatives are allowed to mount the cart and say farewell.

When the time is up – that is to say about a quarter of an hour – the priest and relations get off the cart, the executioner covers the eyes and faces of the prisoners with their caps, and lashes the horses that draw the cart, which slips from under the men's feet. In this way they remain all hanging together.

You often see friends and relations tugging at the hanging men's feet so that they should die quicker and not suffer.

The bodies and clothes of the dead belong to the executioner. If relatives wish for them they must buy them from him. Any bodies that have no friends to bury them are sold to surgeons to be cut up.

You see the most amusing scenes with the messengers the surgeons have sent for the bodies. People in the crowd who hate them often fight them.

These scenes are most interesting – the noise and the muddle is amazing. It can all be seen from rows of seats built near the gibbet.

9 Widow's woe

Not all women wept when they were widowed by the hangman. There is a terribly true tale told about Dick Hughes. On his way to the gallows in 1709 he happened to meet his wife. She climbed on to the cart with him, as she was allowed to do, and they had a chat that really upset her. It went like this…

But, let's face it, it was a nice thought – and she could always use the rope as a washing line, couldn't she?

10 Horrible hooligans

Young men have always caused trouble in London. In the Middle Ages teenage boys learned a trade by becoming a student with a craftsman – the boys were called 'apprentices' and they were a lively lot.

For a start, apprentices from one trade would fight with apprentices in another trade – a bit like rival football supporters today.

In the 1200s a report said...

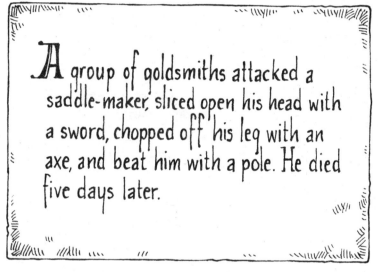

A group of goldsmiths attacked a saddle-maker, sliced open his head with a sword, chopped off his leg with an axe, and beat him with a pole. He died five days later.

Of course they weren't always serious attacks. One apprentice took his bow and fired his arrows into a crowd of people ... for a laugh. He killed an innocent person who probably didn't see the joke.

The law officers didn't have police cars or helicopters, but they did have one power that today's police do not have. What could the law do to you around 1250 that it can't do today?

a) Take all your clothes away so you can't leave the house.

b) Take your doors and windows out so you can't hide your crimes.

c) Take your food away and starve you till you behave yourself.

Answer: **b)** A butcher called William Cok, in Cockes Lane, had 11 doors and five windows removed by the law. Bet that left him without a sausage.

The loathsome London quiz

1 Isambard Kingdom Brunel checked his dad's Thames tunnel using a 'Diving Bell' – a large bell with seats inside that was lowered into the water. Who did he take with him?

a) His mum
b) His dad
c) Queen Victoria

2 In 1605 Guy Fawkes plotted to blow up King James in Parliament. But 18 years before that there was a plot to blow up Queen Elizabeth I. Where?

a) On her throne
b) On her toilet
c) In her bed

Tinkle Tinkle

Tick Tick!

3 In 1780 Londoners believed there was a plot to destroy London, far worse than the Guy Fawkes plot. What was it?

a) To bomb London from hot air balloons
b) To flood London
c) To blow up London with bombs fastened to dogs

4 In 1768 some London soldiers killed rioters in 'The Massacre of St George's Fields'. William Allen was killed. What had he done?

a) Thrown a stone at a magistrate
b) Passed a stone to his friend who threw it at a magistrate
c) Nothing

5 In 1829 Robert Peel formed the London police force. Hundreds of men joined – but half of them were soon sacked. Why?

a) They spent too much time getting drunk.

b) They spent too much time picking on small people and refused to arrest big burglars.

c) They kept trying to arrest posh people when their real job was to arrest poor people.

6 In 1850 Ann Wood went to court. The judge said, 'If you wanted to do it, why didn't you do it and get it done with?' What had Ann Wood tried to do?

a) Keep her slum house clean

b) Drown her cat's kittens

c) Drown herself

7 If you saw Horny Winkle's Horse in Victorian London, what would you see?

a) A beef and rhubarb pie served as a birthday treat

b) A rough children's game

c) A torture machine that forced your feet into your mouth

8 Colonel Thomas Blood almost got away with stealing Charles II's crown jewels from the Tower in 1671. Who may have helped him?

a) King Charles II

b) Rocky the Raven

c) Benny the Beefeater

72

9 In the early 1800s a group called 'The Flying Dustmen' made a good living. How?

a) Stealing teeth from corpses to dentists to make false teeth

b) Stealing vacuum cleaners

c) Stealing dust

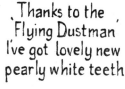

Thanks to the 'Flying Dustman' I've got lovely new pearly white teeth

Ask your Dentist for Dead Man's Molars®

10 On 3 January 1804 Francis Smith was guilty of an unusual crime in Hammersmith. What did he do?

a) He rode a pig down Hammersmith High Street and was charged with speeding.

b) He shot the Hammersmith Ghost dead.

c) He was sleepwalking with no clothes on and walked into a meeting of the Mothers' Union.

Answers:

1a) It was a dangerous and filthy job. But Dad, Marc Brunel, was too ill to do it so 21-year-old Isambard went. His brave mother went to keep an eye on him.

2c) In 1587 Michael Moody, an Irishman, planned to put gunpowder under Queen Elizabeth's bed in her London palace. Frizzled Lizzie. With Elizabeth dead her cousin, Mary, Queen of Scots, would take the throne. Elizabeth was so shocked she signed Mary's death warrant.

3b) The Londoners were afraid of a Catholic rebellion. Word went around that there were tens of thousands of Catholic soldiers hiding in tunnels under the city. When the rebellion started the soldiers would pop out.

Other Catholics would blow up the banks of the Thames to flood London – and flood the tens of thousands of soldiers? Doesn't make a lot of sense. But many potty people in London believed it.

4c) A stone was thrown at magistrate Samuel Gillam. The soldiers set out to catch the stone-thrower – a man in a red waistcoat. The man in red ran away. Guardsman Donald Maclean trapped William Allen in the back yard of an inn. He was wearing a red waistcoat. William said, 'This is my father's inn and I am working here. I've been here all morning.' Maclean didn't believe him. First he stabbed young Will with his bayonet then finished him off with a bullet. But William had been telling the truth. He was not the man who had thrown the stone. Oooops!

5a) Mr Peel's police were not very popular. Two had been killed by the end of 1830. Posters were put up in London streets telling people that the police were armed with weapons from the Tower of London. Kids called them nasty names like 'Raw Lobsters', 'Blue Monsters', 'Bloody Police', and 'Blue Devils'. Poor people pelted them with bricks and ginger-beer bottles. No wonder the unpopular police popped into pubs for pints whenever they had the chance.

dejected inspector   crestfallen constable   sorrowful sergeant   plastered P.C.

6c) Ann Wood jumped in a canal and tried to kill herself. A policeman had to rescue her and then take her to court. That was a nuisance. The judge was angry with her. Instead of showing her some pity he told her she should have done a proper job. 'Why did you not get under the water and make an end of it, instead of giving us all this trouble and bother?' Nice man.

7b) Horny Winkle's Horse is played by two groups of boys – girls couldn't do it because of their long skirts. One group bends over and makes a bridge of their backs – like a long horse. The other group of boys jump on their backs and ride them. As they do so they chant:

CHARLEY KNACKERS ONE, TWO, THREE

(No … I am not making this up. They really did play this game.)

The riders ride till the 'horse' collapses. Then it's the turn of the other group to be the 'horse' and be ridden. (Try this with about nine of your friends – if you have half a brain between the ten of you.)

8a) Blood made friends with the keeper of the jewels and got himself invited to dinner. He tied up the keeper, stuffed some jewels down his trousers and rode off.

Blood was caught but said, 'I will speak to no one but King Charles II himself'. The King forgave him and gave him a pension of £500 a year. Lucky Blood. But why would the King do that? Some people believe Charles II set up the whole thing – stealing his own jewels and selling them.

9c) In Islington Mr Lacock paid the council £750. In return he was allowed to collect all the dust and ashes from the houses. His team of poor women and children gathered it in carts. They then took out the cinders and sold them for half the price of coal, and the rest was sold to make bricks. But there was a dangerous gang who went around pinching the dust – a gang known as 'The Flying Dustmen'. One of the thieves, Charles Fox, was caught stealing dust and beaten up.

A DUSTED-UP DUSTY DUSTMAN

10b) People of Hammersmith were complaining about a ghost wandering the dark streets, so Francis Smith armed himself with a pistol and set out to track it down. Sure enough he saw a pale figure wandering along the road. He pulled out his pistol and shot it. But the pale figure was a brick-maker, Thomas Millwood, wearing a white smock and covered in light brick dust. He died. Francis gave himself up to the police and asked to be hanged. He spent a year in prison and was then set free. Let's hope Tom's ghost didn't return to haunt him.

London language

People in most big cities have their own way of talking. People from the East End of London – Cockneys – made up their own slang words. Their friends could understand them but not many other people could. As one villainous Victorian said…

THE POLICE DON'T UNDERSTAND US AT ALL. IT WOULD BE A PITY IF THEY DID

The Cockneys used a few tricks to make new words – they spelled words backwards…

TOP O' REEB?

SEY!

'Cool him' meant 'Look at him' – a warning when the police were around.

VERY HANDY IF YOU WERE DOING SOMETHING 'DAB'

Sometimes they'd just make up words…

DO YOU TUMBLE MY BARRIKIN?

…which means 'Do you understand me?'

Ridiculous rhymes

But the most famous Cockney trick is when they choose a rhyme for the word. So your 'north' was your 'north and south' – your 'mouth'.

If your dentist told you to 'open your north', or your teacher told you to, 'shut your north', then you may be a bit mixed up. That's how it must have been for the poor police in Victorian London.

Could you help the *namecilop* who arrested this man?

Modern London timeline

1763 The hat makers go on the rampage round Southwark having riots against the government. They call themselves the 'Gang of Hatters'. Ooooh – scary! Imagine them marching and crying, 'Freedom ... or I'll flatten you with my flat cap.'

1780 Lord George Gordon leads the Gordon Riots in London to attack Catholics. One victim is Catholic Mr Malo who owns a silk factory. The mob wreck his home and throw his furniture on to a bonfire. Mr Malo's canaries are stolen. Some people want them as pets. The mob decide they are 'Catholic' canaries – so they are thrown on to the fire, screaming ... not singing but singeing.

1790 The London Monster is caught – the man who stuck a spike in 500 London ladies' bottoms is locked up. No more knifed knickers. Sales of copper petticoats fall.[1]

1820 The Cato Street Conspiracy. A group of workers plot to kill the government – a bit like Guy Fawkes but with swords and pistols instead of gunpowder. They pretend to set

ANGRY HATTERS

WHY CAN'T YOU GET A GUY FAWKES LIKE NORMAL PEOPLE?

ABOUT TIME TOO! HE WAS GIVING US ALL A BAD NAME

1 No joke! Tailors offered to sell ladies knife-proof armour to wear under their skirts. Step–Clank! Step–Clank!

☠ THE HORRIBLE ☠ HIGHLIGHTS OF LONDON

① London Bridge
This is where they stuck the heads of traitors on poles. The message is clear: 'Look out!'

② Tower of London
A palace of pleasure turned to a place of pain. Twisted torture and blood-soaked beheadings, stabbings, drowning and smotherings. Nice.

③ The Old Bailey
Court for villains who are caught. It used to house Newgate prison with the gallows outside. A place to hang around.

④ King's Cross Station
Why were kings cross? Maybe their trains were late! Some say warrior Queen Boudica was buried under platform 8.

⑤ The Globe Theatre
Shakespeare's pleasant plays performed here, along with bloody baiting of bulls and bears. Not now. All's well that ends well!

⑥ Regent's Park
The zoo where snakes were once fed with live rabbits so vile Victorian visitors could see bunny bitten. Hiss-terical!

THE HORRIBLE HIGHLIGHTS OF LONDON

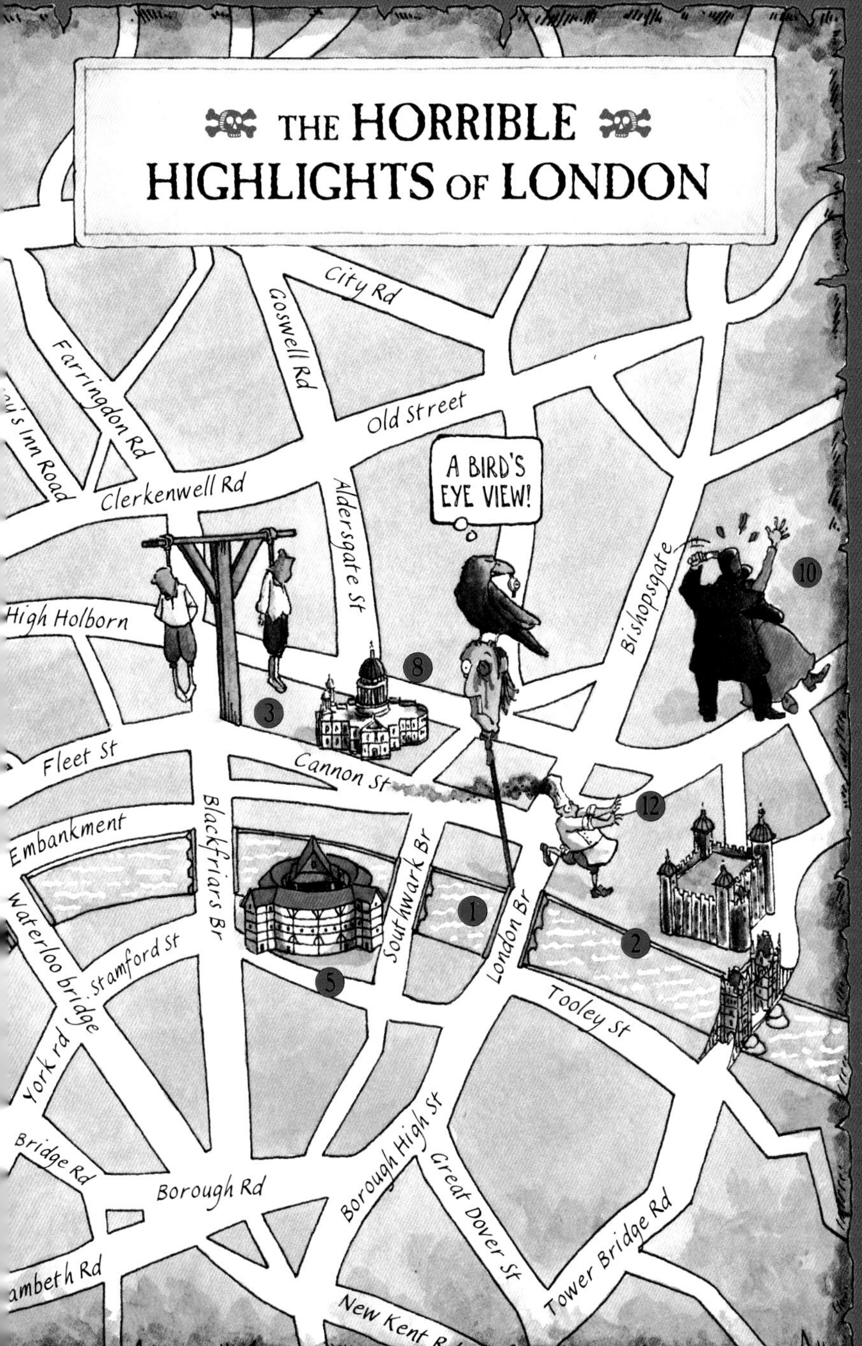

7 Whitehall

Charles I got chopped outside the Banqueting Hall. For a while old Whitehall would be red hall with gutters full of gore. Wipe your feet.

8 St Paul's

The churchyard was a great place for doing deals, watching street amusements, being cheated and getting your pocket picked. Raves on graves.

9 Houses of Parliament

In 1605 villains crept into the basement to blow it up but poor Guy Fawkes was caught. Now the villains are all upstairs.

10 Whitechapel

In Durward Street, 1888, London's greatest villain cut his first throat. The man they call Jack the Ripper. He was never caught. Ooo-er!

11 10 Downing Street

Once a place where people paid to watch cockerels rip each other apart. Now ministers meet there ... to rip each other apart.

12 Pudding Lane

This is where the Great Fire started and cleaned up filthy London's wooden houses. An ember to remember.

up a coffee shop in Cato Street – in fact their weapons are hidden in the loft. The police arrive before the plot is carried out. The plotters fight desperately.

1858 'The Great Stink' – when the suffocating smell of poo in the Thames half chokes the people in Parliament.

1863 The first underground trains – when the smoke of the steam trains half chokes the passengers!

1888 Jack the Ripper stalks the streets of London – then vanishes as suddenly as he appeared. (Or as SHE appeared. It could have been Jill the Ripper, some say.)

1901 Queen Victoria dies. The streets of London are jammed as people say goodbye to a fat old queen and goodbye to a loathsome age in London.

1944 In the Blitz of the Second World War over 40,000 people died in London – about the same number that died during the plague.

Awful execution

The 1700s were the days of the first popular newspapers. Put the riots and the newspapers together and what have you got? Some pretty gruesome reading…

The *HIGH STANDARD* London Edition

GREEN SLAYERS SWING TOGETHER

From Miss Green to Stepney Green the savage seven met their end at the end of a rope this morning. Gallows were specially built so all seven callous killers could swing together. It won't bring Miss Green back to life but she'll be happy in heaven.

Last month Alderman William Beckford – known as Becks – advertized for coal-haulers to do the work of the Thames coal-haulers who were on strike. These muscle men cart the coals from ships to shore. Ten horrible haulers marched to 'The Roundabout Tavern'

where top Becks supporter John Green lived. The strike leader said at the time, 'We plan to cut him to pieces and hang him from his own inn sign.'

But the strikers were driven off with gunfire and three coal-haulers were shot dead. The others turned to Green's sister and she was torn to death. 'We never meant to – we just gave her a bit of a pull and she sort of fell apart,' one of the strikers said. But the judge didn't believe the cruel coalman and all seven were sentenced to die this morning.

The judge didn't hang about – but the haulers will. They'll be covered in tar and hung in cages as a lesson to the others.

Sailors have been doing the work of the coal-haulers so now the violence has turned on them. Sailor John Beatty was stabbed to death in the latest outbreak. Posh Becks said, 'The army is now arresting the ring-leaders and there will be more hangings before the month is out. The gallows will groan with my message. You don't mess with Becks.'

As they say in this part of London: that's entertainment!

One of the savage seven

William Beckford made a fortune from slave trading – he wasn't going to suffer strikes from coal-haulers.

He went on to become Lord Mayor of London.

The Cato killings

If a poor policeman had written a letter about the Cato Street events it might have looked pretty gruesome. Maybe he would scramble the letters of the disgusting words so his mother wouldn't be too horrified.

Horrible Histories warning: Do NOT try to unscramble the words in this report...

Dear Mum,

Still enjoying life as a London policeman – a 'Bow Street Runner'. I have the full inside story of the Cato Street Plot. I've just changed some of the disgusting words because I know you're a weak old lady and I don't want you to be shocked.

It all started on 22 February 1820. Rebel leader Arthur Thistlewood saw an article in the paper saying all the government were going to have dinner in Grosvenor Square. He decided to lead his gang and kill them all. The beast! Thistlewood said their heads would be FLED OF POP and stuck on poles. They would be carried around the slums of London to start the revolution.

Only 27 men agreed to join the gang of SURE MR RED. On 23 February the plotters met in the loft above the Cato Street stable. Little did they know a spy was watching them from the pub across the road. We police moved in to arrest them. (Don't worry, Mum, I stayed at the back.)

One of our police officers, Richard Smithers, moved forward to make the arrests but Thistlewood BATS BED him with his WORDS. What a hero – I hope I'll be my Mum's hero one day – just not a dead one.

Smithers cried, 'Oh God, I am . . .' but we'll never know what he was, because he died before he finished the sentence. Wonder what it was? God, I am hungry? God, I am sorry I left my suit of armour at home? Or, God, I am trying to think of some famous last words but I am going to die before I get to say them?

Anyway, yesterday, 1 May 1820, the five leaders were hanged – very clumsily. Thistlewood GLUT DREGS for a few minutes. Ings suffered most and the hangmen pulled his legs and LENT DRAGS him to finish him off. Then each man was A HEED BED. Crowds flocked to Cato Street to see the BAD STONE OILED floor.

Ladies climbed the steep steps into the loft even though it meant showing their UNWED REAR.

Watching the horror was a young writer called CHILDREN'S CAKES! He said it was the most disgusting thing he's ever seen. Me? I enjoyed it!

Your loving son

Edmund

Did you know … will you ever know…?

The Cato Street plotters were beheaded after they were hanged. The masked man who cut off the heads did a very neat job. The mob who watched decided he must be the doctor Thomas Wakeley. That night they went round to Wakeley's house for revenge – they set fire to the house and he was badly hurt – though not as badly hurt as the headless Cato killers.

Was Wakeley the headsman? Will we ever know?

Horrible hangmen

Executing people is a nasty job. You probably wouldn't want to do it … yes, all right, you wouldn't mind lopping off your history teacher's head for the crime of giving too much homework. But MOST people wouldn't fancy being an executioner. So the men who DID get the job were a little odd.

Here are some of the foulest facts – so foul that we've had to remove the most disgusting bits and put numbers in instead. Decide what you think the missing words are … just think of it as a piece of history homework.

If you are not very bright – or if you are a teacher attempting this – then here are the words … but not in the right order, of course.

Gouged, Executed, Sacked, Stabbed, Rioted, Jumped, Chopped, Whipped, Hanged, Haunted, Wriggled

The first hangman we know about was called Cratwell. In 1538 Cratwell was (1) at Clerkenwell. He stole from a booth at St Bartholomew's fair.

Edward Dennis took part in the Gordon Riots of 1780 but kept his job of hangman and executed 30 of the people who had (2). Six years later he retired and was given a fine robe by the mayor – Dennis sold it.

In 1685 Jack Ketch became one of London's worst-ever executioners. He bungled the execution of the Duke of Monmouth and was (3). But the next hangman, Pascha Rose, was a burglar. Ketch got his job back so he could hang Rose.

In 1714 John Price took the job. In the navy he'd been (4) and his wounds were pickled to make them more painful. He was London hangman for a year but then he attacked a woman pie-seller and (5) one of her eyes. She died. He was executed.

John Thrift was hangman from 1735 till 1752. A crowd gathered outside his house one night to insult him. He ran out and (6) one. The judge set Thrift free to execute again. Thrift was too kind-hearted at times. He almost fainted when he had to behead some rebels in 1745 and he was (7) by the people he'd killed.

Jack Hooper was next and he was known as 'The Laughing Hangman' because he joked with victims on the way to the scaffold. He liked to give the crowds a laugh too. When he (8) the ears off Sir Peter Stranger he waved them at the crowd. He went on to slit Stranger's nose.

Hooper liked to drink a lot before he (9) people. Once he was so drunk he tried to hang the priest who was there to pray for the prisoner. He probably laughed.

William Calcraft liked a laugh too. He executed a boy aged nine in 1832 but did it clumsily. The boy (10) on the end of a short rope so Calcraft (11) on his back to finish him off.

Hangman. A good job? No. A bit ropey in fact.

Did you know…?

Being a hangman could be a dangerous job.

John Meff was due to be hanged in 1717. But the hangman owed a lot of money and the law officers went to his house to take his furniture and sell it, so the hangman missed the hanging.

The mob had been looking forward to seeing Meff swing. They were furious. So they went around to the hangman's house and beat him to death.

Meanwhile, you are probably wondering what happened to Meff.

Meff was pardoned and sent to a prison colony in America. On the way his ship was attacked by pirates and he was marooned on a deserted island off the American coast. He found a canoe and paddled to America.

In 1721 he returned to London (on a ship – he didn't paddle his canoe). But his luck ran out. He was arrested and hanged. This time the hangman turned up and finished him off.

The bad old days...

A lot of people talk about 'the good old days'. But there wasn't much good about the old days in London.

Even a hundred years ago most people had miserable and dirty lives.

• Servants like cooks and maids often slept in the kitchen because their bosses didn't think they needed a bedroom.

• In the middle of the housing areas there were 6,000 pig pens and slaughter houses.[1]

• Londoners were afraid that fresh air and baths would harm them – so they got very little of either.

• Most people only had one set of clothes and wore them all the time. We don't know how often those clothes were washed – some people probably *never* washed their clothes.

• Coal fires filled the air with soot, turned the houses black and choked the Londoners when fog turned into sooty fog: smog.

The smell of the people and the houses would be sickening to us. Germs must have loved London. Diseases spread quickly and killed many – mostly the poor people who were weak from eating bad food and from overwork.

Slaughterhouses

If you wanted fresh meat then you had to keep your sheep, cattle and pigs in the city and kill them there. (There were no fridges.)

No one wanted to eat the guts so they were thrown into the gutters to be washed away – till a law in the 1300s put a stop to that.

1 There was even a story that a herd of wild pigs lived in the sewers under Hampstead. That wasn't true!

But the poor people of London didn't get the best meat. They could only afford the mouldy scraps that were days old.

An American visitor described an open-air butcher stall in 1899...

Not only is the worker poorly fed, but he is filthily fed. I stood outside a butcher's and watched a horde of housewives turning over the trimmings and scraps and shreds of beef and mutton – stuff we'd call dog-meat in the States. With filthy hands they raked and pawed and scraped the mess about to get the best their coppers could buy. I kept my eye on one disgusting bit of mutton, and watched it go through the hands of over twenty women. At last it was picked up by a timid little woman whom the butcher bullied into taking it. All day long this heap of scraps was added to and taken away from; the dust and dirt of the street falling upon it, flies settling on it, and the dirty fingers turning it over and over.

'ERE, LOOK AT THIS SLIMY LUMP OF GRISTLE

LOVELY

Scrummy! Still, it could have been worse for the woman. She could have been the sheep she went off to eat.

London's lousy jobs

London is the place to go for a job – an odd job … or a very odd job.

In the 1800s children made a poor living by collecting and selling the dog-ends of cigars. The streets were muddy and covered in horse-poo. So a five-year-old crossing-sweeper would make a few pennies by clearing the way for posh people.

But these weren't the worst jobs you could do in loathsome London. Here are a few from the past. Your school careers adviser will NOT tell you about these terrible top ten jobs. Here they are in reverse horrible horder…

10 Head tar man

When a traitor was executed in London he was beheaded and cut into quarters. The heads were stuck on poles at the gates in the city walls, at the Tower of London, at Westminster or on London Bridge. This went on till 1746 when the last head to go on show was that of Francis Townley, a rebel who wanted the Scottish Bonnie Prince Charlie on the English throne. For a few pennies you could rent a telescope to get a good close look at his dead head. Yeuch!

These heads rotted, of course, and were pecked to bits by birds. So they were boiled in salt or painted with tar to make them last. Head painting. Could YOU do it?

> PAINTING FOUL, STINKING DEAD THINGS WITH REVOLTING BLACK STUFF? ARE YOU KIDDING?

9 Running patterer

London people loved a good murder. They loved crime so much they would pay to read more about it. In the 1800s a running patterer would sell you a printed paper with all the latest gory stories. At an execution he would sell you the dying speech of the murderer – before he had been hanged.

If there were no good stories then what did the running patterer do? He made them up! The patterer invented a story and sold it on the streets. One patterer said…

> *I killed the Duke of Wellington twice, had Prince Louis assassinated twice (once with a bullet, once with a knife) and broke Prince Albert's arm … or was it his leg?*

Another patterer said he'd given Queen Victoria triplets: 'I did think of poisoning the Pope but the Catholics would have given me a beating.'

It's just like the newspapers of the twenty-first century – if there's no news they make it up!

Some of their poems were dreadful rhymes. When John Thurtell murdered William Weare in 1823 he was sent to be hanged. In court he made a curious speech that ended...

PLEASE DON'T HAVE ME EXECUTED BECAUSE IT WOULD REALLY UPSET MY PARENTS

His parents must have been really upset when the patterers sold John's story at his execution with this vile verse...

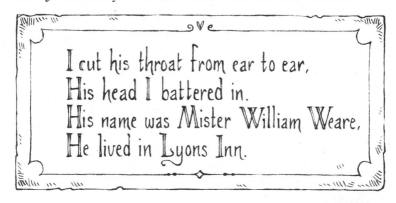

I cut his throat from ear to ear,
His head I battered in.
His name was Mister William Weare,
He lived in Lyons Inn.

8 Toilet cleaner

You may think London toilets can make you ill. But a hundred years ago those toilets could kill you. The poo gave off a gas, and if that gas filled your house it could choke you. Or, sometimes, a spark could cause the gas to explode. This is extra deadly if you are sitting on the toilet at the time. (So remember – never smoke in the school toilets.)

Small children were often sent into toilet pits because they could fit down the narrow pipes. They were expected to clean them ... and you complain when your parents ask you to clean their car?

The toilet-cleaning kids often choked on the gas. In 1849 a report into a toilet explosion read...

Explosions happened in two separate places. In the first the men had the skin peeled off their faces and their hair singed. Further along the second lamp created an explosion that burnt the hair and face of the person holding it.

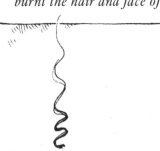

In 1731 six prisoners in Newgate escaped into the sewers. Four got away. The skeletons of the other two were found many years later.

What a way to go. Or waterway to go...

7 Watercress seller

An honest job – but a miserable one.

Little girls would be sent on to the streets by their parents to sell watercress – green stuff that cooks used to decorate boring meals.

The watercress had to be fresh – no freezers to keep it green and crisp. So the little girls had to go out every day in all weather to sell their cress.

As one eight-year-old child said…

> *When the snow is on the ground I bears the cold – you must, so I puts my hands under my shawl, though it hurts them to take hold of the cresses, especially when we takes 'em to the pump to wash 'em. No, I never see any children crying – it's no use.*

6 Lurker

If you can read this you can probably write. If you can write then you could become a 'lurker'. A lurker knew how to copy the handwriting of rich people. He would then write letters that were supposed to come from those rich people. You know the sort of thing…

My Dearest Lady Mary
I am sending you this poor man because I know you can help him. He has thirteen children and is out of money but I could only afford five pounds. If you can give him a little cash then his family will not starve this week.
Your dear friend
Sir Peter Popplecrump

One famous lurker forged the name of a judge. He was brought before the judge.

Of course there are still lurkers lurking today. Some young lurkers forge letters from their parents so they don't have to do horrible things at school … things like cross-country running, or a detention for blowing your nose in class. Shocking.

A *Horrible Histories* reader, like you, must never be caught doing such a thing. (You may *do* it … but you must never be *caught*.)

5 Mudlark

Men, women and children would wait for the tide to go out and then step into the thick mud on the banks of the River Thames. They would plod along and use their fingers and toes to search for anything that might have been dropped from ships – scraps of rope, coal, wood, iron and copper – anything they could sell.

Even in bitter winter weather you could see them wading through the mud. One boy said…

It was very cold in winter to stand in the mud without shoes. But if I didn't find anything I'd starve until the next low tide. A lot of lads have to do it. We're nearly all fatherless, and our mothers are too poor to keep us; so we take to it because we have nothing else to do.

Some mudlarks collected old bones and sold them to factories to make soap. Some collected coal. When a reporter saw a woman with a bag of coal he said it would keep her nice and warm that night. She laughed at him…

Make a fire with the coals I pick up? People like me don't have coal fires, mister. Anything does for a fire for me and my old man – we burn cinders, driftwood, anything. But coals is money and we can't afford to burn money.

4 Coiner

Take a coin, smear it in grease and press it into some damp plaster. Take the coin out and what have you got? An image of the coin. A 'mould'.

Do that for both sides of the coin.

Now melt down a cheap spoon and pour the metal into the mould. Open the mould and you have a new coin.

The next bit is tricky. You need to 'plate' it to make it shiny like a real coin. The Victorians used nitric acid, sulphuric acid and cyanide – all deadly poisons – to give their fake coins a shiny silver coat. Don't do it the Victorian way!

Next 'slum' the shiny coin – make it look well-used by rubbing it with soot and oil.

Then spend it.

Of course, Victorian coiners would go to prison for life if they were caught. Before the 1830s coiners had their hands lopped off or were hanged.

Top three London jobs

You don't fancy forging coins or selling cress? You will when you look at the other horrible jobs you could be forced to do. Here are the top three.

Remember, if you DON'T fancy these jobs then you will just have to starve to death…

3 Dredger

If you don't mind handling dead and rotting bodies then why not become a dredger?

Lots of people seemed to end up in the Thames – dead. And Londoners didn't want their river blocked up with shore-to-shore corpses. So they offered a reward to anyone who dragged a body from the river.

The dredgers set out in their little rowing boats and hauled the bodies from the water.

The first thing to do is go through the pockets to see if there is anything worth pinching. Then go to the nearest police station, hand over the body and collect your reward.

Of course, it could get messy. If a body has been in the river too long then arms and legs could drop off as you try to haul it in.

2 Tosher

Want to make some extra pocket money? Become a 'tosher'. Here's how...

Find a sewer – you know, the big underground drains that all the toilets empty into.

Find the place where the sewer flows into the River Thames and walk in the entrance.

People sometimes drop valuable things down toilets and down drains in the street – jewellery or coins – all you have to do is stick your hands in the fast-flowing poo and find the stuff. (It's known as 'tosh' and you are a 'tosher'.)

Easy.

A Victorian writer, Henry Mayhew, said...

These toshers may be seen dressed in long greasy velvet coats with vast pockets, and their legs are covered by dirty canvas trousers, and any old slops of shoes that are only fit for wading through the mud.

WHAT A LOAD OF TOSH

LOVELY

If there was a ship close by then the toshers would try to steal the copper that covered its bottom.

The toshers loved to tell horrible stories. This is a story that one tosher told Henry Mayhew. Mayhew seemed to believe it and he wrote it down. Of course the tosher COULD have been lying. What do you think?

When I was a tosher I often saw a hundred rats in a swarm. And they are whoppers in the sewers, I can tell you. Them were water rats too, and they is far more ferociouser than any other rats.

They'd think nothing of attacking a man. Usually they runs away and gets out of the road. But if they find they can't get out of his way, nohow, they'll turn on him.

I knows one chap that was tackled by the rats in the sewer. They bit him awfully. You must have heard about it? Some boatmen were rowing past the end of the sewer when they heard him scream. If they hadn't rescued him the rats would have killed him sure enough.

> Don't you remember hearing about the man found in the sewers twelve years ago? Oh, you must have done. The rats ate every bit of him and left nothing but bones!

A true tale? Or do you smell a rat?

1 Pure finder

Yes, it's number one – the top London job.

As you know, leather comes from the skins of dead animals. But once that skin is stripped off the animal it starts to go hard – no one wants to wear shoes that feel like they're made of iron.

So the leather goes to a 'tanner' who works on it to make it soft. How did the London tanners do this 200 years ago? You don't want to know. Just skip to the next section.

You do? Fine. Just don't eat your tea as you read this.

The tanner would rub in doggie poo. (I did warn you.) You would not find many tanners who would bite their nails – and you would not find many people happy to shake hands with a tanner.

Now tanners were busy men – no time to go round the streets collecting doggie doo-doo. That's where the 'pure finder' came in.

Pure finders went round the streets and scooped up the dog droppings. Nice if you had a shovel – messy if you had to use your bare hands.

Off you go to that top London job. Pure finder.

Terrible for tots to teens

Orphans had a terrible time in 1700s London. They were sent to a 'workhouse' where they had to work hard for nasty nibbles of nosh.

The workhouses were happy to send them out to work in people's homes as servants – and some of the poor kids must have been glad to go to a better life.

Others went to slavery … or death.

Elizabeth Brownrigg

The bruising, beating Brownrigg beast had several penniless girls working for her as servants in her own home. Here are ten terrible things to do to a girl. Which of these did Bullying Brownrigg do to Mary Clifford?

1 Beat her with a broom or a horse-whip

2 Made her sleep on a mat in a coal hole, in the cold with no blanket, only her thin dress

3 Fed her on bread and water – and not enough of either

4 Tied a chain around her neck, pulled it till it almost choked her and fastened it to a door for 12 hours

5 Tied her hands with a cord and pulled the cord through a hook in the ceiling before whipping her

6 Grabbed her by the cheeks and pulled the skin till the girl's eyes began to bleed

7 Cut her tongue with a pair of scissors

8 Whipped her till she bled then made her bathe in cold water

9 Whipped her so hard Brownrigg had to stop for a rest to get her breath back

10 Dipped her head into a pail of water

Mary Clifford was rescued by the police but died two days later. Brownrigg, her husband and her son were charged with murder. They were hanged in 1767. As they were led to their execution the crowds yelled at them…

You will go to hell and the devil himself will come and fetch you!

After her hanging Brownrigg's body was cut up by the doctors and her skeleton was hung up in Surgeons' Hall.

Sarah Metyard

Would a horrible hanging put you off cruelty to children? It didn't deter Sarah Metyard and her daughter. In 1768, just a year after the Brownrigg hangings, the Metyards were charged with murdering a workhouse girl…

Little Anne Naylor tried to run away from the miserable Metyards so they beat her, then tied her to a door so she couldn't sit down or stand up. They left her like this for three days with no food.

Other serving girls found her strung up on the door and ran to Sarah Metyard. The reports told the story…

Wrong!

The murderous Metyards had got away with it.

Anne's sister spotted some of Anne's clothes in the house and threatened to report the miserable Metyards. They strangled her and got rid of the body. They thought they had got away with that too.

For four years no one suspected them and poor Anne was buried and forgotten.

Then suddenly they were arrested and sent to trial. What had gone wrong?

a) The ghost of Anne reported her own murder to the police.

b) Sarah and her daughter argued and the daughter reported her to the police.

c) A servant looked in Anne's room and found a four-year-old finger that the killers had forgotten.

Answer: **b)** Sarah started to beat her daughter the way they had beaten Anne. The fed-up daughter reported her mother for murder – but they were both hanged. Sarah fainted on her way to the scaffold and they could not wake her up. They hanged her anyway so she probably woke up dead.

105

The baby farmers

Babies from poor families could be too much trouble to care for. So, in the 1700s and 1800s, many parents sent their babies off to child-minders they called 'baby farmers'.

Some farmers care for their animals – some can be cruel.

Baby farmers were the same – some kind, some cruel. Some baby farmers kept the kids quiet by drugging them with opium.

In 1750 Dr Cadogan said…

Thomas Coram built a hospital for children and in 1742 he said…

In the 1870s the bodies of babies were found lying around the streets of Lambeth. They were the victims of a baby farmer, Margaret Waters. Police found another five children, sick and dying, at her house.

She was hanged.

Did you know…?

London kids have played some disgusting games. One Middle Ages game was to crawl under the scaffold where someone had been beheaded. The nasty nippers would then scrape up any blood they could find there. Foul fun.

Teenagers were no better in the 1800s. When they got bored they played a disgusting game.

> *Horrible Histories* note: Do NOT try this at home.[1] Do NOT pick on innocent wrinklies in the street.

Here's what Victorian teens did…

 ## The egg and soot game

You need: Eggs, soot, a bucket, a l-o-n-g brush

To make:
Break two or three eggs into the bucket. Add a cup full of soot. Whisk it all together.

To play:
a) You need a couple of friends. Take your bucket of egg-soot into the street with the brush in it.
b) Your friend stops a posh old person in the street and asks them the time. As they look at their watch take your long brush and slap the egg-soot across their face.
c) Run.

---

1 Wait till you get to school and try it on the wrinkly teachers. When they threaten to expel you then just say you were conducting an historical experiment.

The egg-soot is horribly messy and hard to wash off.

Of course you have to be sure you DON'T try this on a young, fit person or they may catch you and give you the beating you deserve.

This disgusting game was popular with posh young men, not scruffy street kids. The scruffy street kids would not waste eggs in that way. They'd eat them.

Waggers and nickers

London could be a cruel place for kids to live. And kids had to be cruel to survive.

In the 1870s a London boy explained to a judge...

At ten we hops the wag; at 13 we nicks things; an' at 16 we bashes the copper.

YOUR HONOUR, HE MEANS THAT AT THE AGE OF TEN THEY PLAY TRUANT, AT 13 THEY START STEALING AND AT 16 THEY ARE BIG ENOUGH TO ASSAULT THE POLICE

And it wasn't only the young truants who made trouble. The ones who stayed at school could cause problems too.

Take the school strikes of the 1880s and 1890s...

Terrible teachers

HERE IS THE NEWS TODAY, 14 OCTOBER 1889. AND TODAY'S MAIN NEWS IS THAT SCHOOLCHILDREN HAVE GONE ON STRIKE IN WOOLWICH, CHARLTON, PLUMSTEAD AND LAMBETH. OUR REPORTER IS AT THE SCENE IN CHARLTON, COME IN ALBERT...

THESE SKIVING SCHOOLKIDS SEEM TO BE PROTESTING ABOUT EVERYTHING FROM BULLYING HEAD-TEACHERS TO HAVING TOO MUCH HOMEWORK. SOME WANT MORE HOLIDAYS AND SOME WANT TO LEAVE SCHOOL AT THE AGE OF 12

SO HOW DID IT ALL START, ALBERT?

I ASKED ONE OF THE PUPILS THAT AND THIS IS WHAT HE SAID...

ONE OF OUR MATES WAS TEN MINUTES LATE AND THE TEACHER GAVE HIM TWENTY STROKES OF THE CANE. THAT'S NOT FAIR, IS IT? WE ALL WALKED OUT WE WENT ROUND THE OTHER SCHOOLS AND THEY JOINED IN. WE WANT THE CANE BANNED

HUNDREDS OF CHILDREN HAVE BEEN MARCHING THROUGH THE STREETS WAVING FLAGS THAT SAY, 'NO CANE!'

AND WHAT WILL HAPPEN TO THEM WHEN THEY GET BACK TO SCHOOL TOMORROW?

And they were.

The striking pupils of 1889 handed a letter to the Director of London schools. It demanded things like free school meals and free school – each pupil paid a penny a day. The Director just laughed at their letter.

The boys who led the strike were lined up in front of the other pupils and beaten – extra hard.

The teachers could not understand how strikes could spring up all over Britain at the same time – there were no mobile phones in 1889 to pass the word around. They thought there must be a schoolboy spy network. One panicking paper, *The Dundee Advertiser*, wrote…

No one knows how word spread so the pupils can all strike at the same time. There has to be a plot. If Britain has secret societies of schoolchildren then the Empire is doomed.

Guess what? Sixty years later the British Empire was finished. Must have been those young rebels, eh?

Suffocating schools

The children who went to school suffered in stuffy classrooms. In 1848 Hector Gavin made a report on health in Bethnal Green. He said one school was especially nasty ... and it wasn't just the terrible teachers.

The St Matthew schools were built in 1846 close to the church, in the north-west corner of the graveyard. The graves are stuffed to overflowing with corpses. There are hundreds of bodies buried under the floor of the church. To keep them fresh, air is allowed to flow under the floor. The air comes out at the end of a passage, right beside the back door of the school. It is also close to the most filthy toilet used by the children. I tried to examine the toilets but was overcome by the smell, the worst sickness I have ever felt in all my visits to unhealthy sites.

There is no water whatever for the children. There is one small heater for the 275 boys and their teacher. In winter most of them freeze. In summer they cannot open the windows because a slaughterhouse is next door to them and the smell of dead cattle makes the children suffer from headaches and sickness.

Teacher terror

Of course it could be terrible being a teacher too.

In the 1890s Sarah-Anne Knobstick ran home to her mother. 'Mummy, Mummy!' she cried, 'Miss Trimmer gave me the cane!'

She showed her little hand to her red-faced, thick-armed mother.

'Did she now,' her mother Katherine Knobstick said. 'We'll see about that.'

Katherine Knobstick marched down to Lirriper Lane Board School, burst through the doors and grabbed hold of Miss Dorothy Trimmer. First she told her what she thought of her – she used language you wouldn't see even in a *Horrible Histories* book. But (to put it politely) she said…

Then she grabbed the teacher by the hair, tore out lumps and punched her to the floor. As the frail teacher whimpered, the mighty boot of Mrs Knobstick pounded her.

The powerful parent was taken to court and fined a huge amount – 40 shillings. But she smirked and said…

Barmy buildings

London is not just the people, of course. It is thousands of old buildings too. Here are some you may like to visit. You can bore everyone around you by telling them these useless facts...

Marble Arch

This was built in 1827 in front of Buckingham Palace to make a grand entrance for the royal carriages. Sadly the dumbo who built it forgot to measure the carriages – they were too wide to get through! The arch was moved down the road in 1851. The only people who are now allowed to pass through Marble Arch are the royal family and the King's Troop Royal Horse Artillery.

The Thames Tunnel

In the 1820s Marc Brunel built a tunnel under the Thames from Rotherhithe to Wapping in London: the world's first tunnel under a river. As the workers dug under the river it began to leak. It let in water – and all the sewage from London's toilets. One massive flood in 1828 killed six workmen. Mark's famous son, Isambard Kingdom Brunel, was caught and dragged out, barely alive. Isambard later had to crawl through the toilet filth to repair the cracks that let the river leak in.[1]

1 The tunnel is still in use as part of the London Underground system.

The Crystal Palace

Queen Victoria's husband, Prince Albert, wanted to show the world how great Britain was. He wanted an exhibition. A massive glass hall was built in Hyde Park. There were some odd problems though.

Enemies of the plan said that it would attract tramps and, anyway, it would blow down in the first strong wind. (It didn't and it didn't.)

The Lincoln MP said Britain didn't want all those foreign people to visit – they might bring a plague with them. They didn't.

Victoria was worried about birds nesting in the trees, inside the glass palace. Would the birdy poo drop on people? Someone said, 'Kill the birds with hawks!'

The shocked Queen decided to let the birds live to poo in the palace.

In 1854 the palace was moved to Sydenham Hill in South London and in 1936 it burned to the ground.

10 Downing Street

This house is the home of prime ministers – but when they lose the job they have to move out … a bit like a hotel manager.

The top MPs – the 'cabinet' – meet there to plot and plan what to do with the taxes they squeeze from the people. Just like William the Conqueror in the Tower in the old days!

On this spot there used to be a 'cock-pit'. No, that was not the place where an aeroplane pilot sat. It was a pit where cockerels fought to the death.

In 1787 a cockerel called Old Trodgon won £200 for a fight at 10 Downing Street – a fortune in those days.

Then the place became a coffee house and a popular place for thieves to meet people who would buy their stolen goods.

So 10 Downing Street was a place for crooks to meet.

The Houses of Parliament

Guy Fawkes tried to destroy Westminster Palace – the old Houses of Parliament – and kill King James in 1605. His ghost must have been happy when it burned down.

In 2003 the teachers at Aberystwyth University tried to work out what would have happened if Guy had lit the fuse. They reckoned...

- The bang would have been big enough to wipe out 25 Houses of Parliament.
- The King and parliament would have been blasted up high into the air ... if they had lived then they would have been killed when they came back down to earth.
- Everything within 30 metres would have been blown apart.
- Every building within 100 metres would have had its roof blown off.
- Flying bricks and tiles could have killed anyone closer than 150 metres.

Westminster Palace was used to store all the tax records of England from the Middle Ages till 1826. The place was stuffed with them. These records were made of wood. In 1834 someone said they'd burn well and keep the place warm. They burned so well they burned the palace down that same year.

Victoria Embankment

A new Houses of Parliament was built by the side of the Thames in 1864–1870. Big mistake, as the river was London's biggest sewer. In summer it stank enough to choke the Members of Parliament.

What to do with poo was always a problem. Most London houses had pits at the bottom of the house where the poo and pee collected. 'Night Soil Men' would empty the sludge from the pits on to carts, carry the muck off and sell it to farmers to spread on their land. It made their crops grow better – poo-rich oats perhaps.

But as London got bigger the Night Soil Men had too far to travel. Toilet pits filled to overflowing.

In 1842 Edwin Chadwick, a social reformer, wrote…

I found the cellars of some houses to be full of night soil, 3 feet (90 cm) deep. I found the back yard covered in night soil from the overflowing toilet. It was 6 inches (15 cm) deep and bricks had to be put down so the house owners could cross with dry shoes.

New drains took the toilet waste into the Thames. So the Thames became London's toilet.

Londoners took drinking water from the Thames. In the 1850s, 30,000 of them died from the disease cholera. Tasty Thames.

The government wouldn't pay the money to have the filth removed – not until the filth came to the government. In 1858 a hot summer made the river really smell. The stench choked the MPs in Parliament, so they decided to pay for proper London drains. It was known as 'The Great Stink'.

Joseph Bazalgette built sewers that took the toilet waste and dumped it down the river near Barking. It was washed out to sea. (Super swimming, then.)

He also built Victoria Embankment to cover a long stretch of sewer. Think of that as you stroll along.

Did you know…?
The clock tower at the end of the new Houses of Parliament is not 'Big Ben'. It's the great bell that is known as Big Ben. And did you also know it cracked in 1859? It was repaired but the crack's still there. It used to take two men 32 hours to wind the clock every week.

The London landmark you'll never see...

The Wembley Tower

In 1889 the French built the Eiffel Tower. In 1896 Sir Edward Watkin planned to build an even taller tower in Wembley. It should have had restaurants, theatres and even a ballroom at the top. (A lot of steps for Cinderella to run down.)

Mr Eiffel, who built the Paris tower, refused to help.

It was half built. Nobody wanted to pay to go up the tower. It started to sink into the marshy ground. The Leaning Tower of Wembley.

It closed in 1899 and was blown up in 1907. The famous old Wembley Stadium was put there instead.

Under London

London may be horrible above the ground, but it can be just as ugly under the surface.

The Victorian Londoners were very superstitious. One preacher, Dr Cuming, said that digging into the ground would be digging into Hell and the Devil would be disturbed. (Even today people say the Underground is Hell, so maybe he was right.)

The first tube trains ran on 10 January 1863 from Paddington to Farringdon. So many people got on at the start that there was no room for anyone to get on at the other stations. Not a lot has changed there, then.

Steam trains were used for 25 years. Of course the tunnels filled with smoke. The railway companies said the smoke was a GOOD thing. If you had a bad chest then tube smoke would clear it. (Yeah, and putting your head on the track would cure your headache.)

Electric trains were first used in 1890. The law said you would be fined £2 if you tried to ride on the roof of an electric train. If you rode on the roof your head would be knocked off. Painful – but at least you'd save two pounds.

Ten terrible tube facts

Here are some foul facts about the Tube you may like to torment your teacher with. Get Sir (or Miss) on a tube and when it enters a tunnel and the lights flicker, then fill their ears with these truly terrible (but useless) facts.

PLEASE, SIR, COULD YOU REARRANGE THE FOLLOWING TEN FACTS INTO ORDER OF USELESSNESS...SCORE 10 FOR 'I-DIDN'T-NEED-TO-KNOW-THAT' TO 1 FOR UTTERLY-AND-MIND-KILLINGLY-USELESS

1 To test the first escalators they used a man called Bumper Harris because Bumper couldn't mangle his feet if it went wrong – he had two wooden legs.[1]

2 The first tube carriages had no windows and buttoned seats so they were known as 'padded cells'.

3 More people commit suicide at King's Cross and Victoria stations than at any other.

4 People who throw themselves under tube trains are called 'one-unders' by the staff. (In New York they call them 'track pizza').

5 The tunnels were cleaned at night by ladies with feather dusters, dustpans and brushes. They were known as 'fluffers'.

6 The two best stations to spot mice scurrying over the lines are Waterloo and Oxford Circus.

7 Nesting pigeons were a nuisance so staff used kestrels and hawks to kill them.

8 Carriages are too small today for most people who travel on the tube. This is because the tunnels were built in the 1860s when people were smaller.

9 Prime Minister Gladstone and Dr Barnardo were the only people ever to have their coffins carried by tube.

But the winner – the most useless fact of all – is:

10 Green grapes cause more accidents on the London Underground than banana skins.

1 Of course no one checked if he had wooden feet too, did they? For all we know brave Bumper could have been wearing his own feet on the end of the wooden legs. Bet you didn't think of that, did you?

Ghostly goings-on...

Of course, the Underground is haunted.

People say there are ghastly ghosts in deserted houses. So there must be sad spooks in deserted stations. The Underground has lots of stations that no one uses today.

Here are some of the scariest and hairiest places to be...

*These stations are closed now – ghost stations in fact.

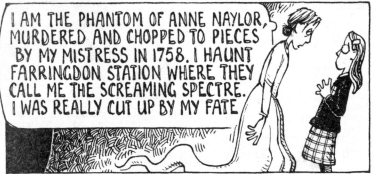

Did you know…?

There is no tube station at Muswell Hill. There was supposed to be, but when they started digging underground they came across a deep pit – full of the skeletons of people buried during the plague.

London ends

London is a terrible place to die. And a place to die terribly. Here are a few of the most horrible.

The Whitefriars Carpenter (around 1820)

He was desperately poor – so poor he had to sell his tools to buy food. And once he'd sold his tools he couldn't find any work. He became poorer and hungrier. Worst of all, he had no friends.

The man decided to kill himself. He had seen how guillotines worked in France. He used his skill to make a machine that would drop a 12 kg stone on to an axe that would cut his throat.

It worked.

His corpse was sent for trial. He was found guilty of suicide. But his horrible death wasn't cruel enough for the jury. They said he didn't deserve a Christian burial. The foreman of the jury said:

He should be flung into a hole at night time, like a dog in a ditch.

His body was pushed into a rough wooden box and buried at midnight in a shallow grave. No one cared. No one cried.

The Spitalfields Children (1883)

If you catch scarlet fever today you will almost certainly survive. If you caught it in Victorian London you could well die. And your poor family could also suffer if you died. A public health inspector called Wrack visited one house where a child had been sick with scarlet fever and wrote this report…

On visiting No. 17, Hope Street, Spitalfields, I found in the room of the second floor the dead body of a child. She had died fifteen days before the time of my visit. The room was occupied by the parents of the dead child and a daughter aged thirteen years. The body was in a rotted state. The father said he could not afford a funeral. Friends had promised to help but had failed to. I pointed out the danger of keeping a dead body so long in the same room where the family lived.

Upon visiting No. 28, Church Street, Spitalfields, on the 5th December last, I found in the second-floor front room the dead body of a child which had died of scarlet fever on the 1st of the month. The body was not in a coffin, and it lay exposed on a table in one corner of the room. The room was occupied as a living and sleeping room by five persons, the father and mother, their child, a girl about three years old, the grandfather and grandmother of the child, who were tailors. The smell on entering the room was most sickening.

The tailors were working in a room with a scarlet fever victim. The person who bought the clothes could catch the disease from them and so it spread.

Mr Wrack made many reports of this sort. In most cases the parents could not afford a funeral.

The government said it had 'no time' to deal with the problem of bodies left to rot in houses.

The Lisson Grove Old Woman (1900)

An American writer, Jack London, visited London ... the city, not his dad ... and wrote about the lives of the poorest people in the slums. His tale of one old woman is gruesome, but true...

In Devonshire Place, Lisson Grove, a short while back an old woman died aged seventy-five. A police officer said that all he found in the room was a lot of old rags covered with fleas and lice. He had got himself smothered with the vermin. The room was in a shocking condition, and he had never seen anything like it. Everything was absolutely covered with fleas.

The doctor said: 'I found the deceased lying across the fireplace on her back. She had a dress and her stockings on. The body was quite alive with vermin, and all the clothes in the room were absolutely grey with insects. The woman was very badly fed and was very skinny. She had sores on her legs from the insect bites, and her stockings were sticking to those sores.'

A man said 'I had the bad luck to see the body of the unhappy woman as it lay in the coffin; she was a mere bundle of skin and bones. Her hair, which was matted with filth, was simply a nest of vermin. Over her bony chest leaped and rolled hundreds, thousands, countless numbers of insects.'

Epilogue

Of course there are a lot of great things to love about London – and this book only has the space to look at the loathsome, not the lovely. Here are three things people have written about London.

Spot the difference…

a) The people of Foster Lane empty their toilet pots out of the windows and cause a nuisance to the people in the street below. The cooks of Bread Street keep animal droppings and rubbish under their counters while a stream of sewage runs down Trinity Lane. Barbers show bowls of blood in their shop windows.

b) No more dreary spectacle can be found on this earth than the whole of the 'awful East' London. The colour of life is grey and drab. Everything is hopeless and dirty. Bath-tubs are totally unknown. The people themselves are dirty. Strange smells come drifting along the greasy wind, and the rain when it falls, is more like grease than water from heaven. The very cobblestones are scummed with grease.

c)

> The murder rate in London has doubled in 12 months to reach one of its highest levels ever. The crimes are getting more brutal. In the final three months of last year there were 61 murders in the capital. Behind each murder there is a tragic story of a family left behind, children left fatherless and wives who are now widows.

They are ALL about London and they are ALL about a Loathsome London. But what is the difference?

a) was written in the year 1212, **b)** was written in 1899 and **c)** was written in 2004.

So some things change – the plague is gone and the sewers work.

Some things haven't changed – the cruelty, the violence, the rats and the lonely lost people.